EARLY CHILDHOOD EDUCATION SERIES
NANCY FILE & CHRISTOPHER P. BROWN, EDITORS
ADVISORY BOARD: Jie-Qi Chen, Cristina Gillanders, Jacqueline Jones,
Kristen M. Kemple, Candace R. Kuby, John Nimmo,
Amy Noelle Parks, Michelle Salazar Pérez, Andrew J. Stremmel, Valora Washington

Pro-Blackness in Early Childhood Education:
Diversifying Curriculum and Pedagogy in K–3 Classrooms
GLORIA SWINDLER BOUTTE, JARVAIS J. JACKSON, SAUDAH N. COLLINS, JANICE R. BAINES, ANTHONY BROUGHTON, & GEORGE LEE JOHNSON

Seven Crucial Conversations in Early Childhood Education: Where Have We Been and Why Does It Matter?
NANCY FILE, NANCY E. BARBOUR, & ANDREW J. STREMMEL, EDS.

Supporting Korean American Children in Early Childhood Education: Perspectives From Mother-Educators
SOPHIA HAN, JINHEE KIM, SOHYUN MEACHAM, & SU-JEONG WEE

Relationship-Based Care for Infants and Toddlers: Fostering Early Learning and Development Through Responsive Practice
SUSAN L. RECCHIA, MINSUN SHIN, & ELENI LOIZOU

Infants and Toddlers at Work: Using Reggio-Inspired Materials to Support Brain Development, Second Edition
ANN LEWIN-BENHAM

Leading Anti-Bias Early Childhood Programs: A Guide to Change, for Change, 2nd Ed.
LOUISE DERMAN-SPARKS, DEBBIE LEEKEENAN, & JOHN NIMMO

We Are the Change We Seek: Advancing Racial Justice in Early Care and Education
IHEOMA U. IRUKA, TONIA R. DURDEN, KERRY-ANN ESCAYG, & STEPHANIE M. CURENTON

Young Investigators:
The Project Approach in the Early Years, 4th Ed.
JUDY HARRIS HELM, LILIAN G. KATZ, & REBECCA WILSON

Emotionally Responsive Teaching: Expanding Trauma-Informed Practice With Young Children
TRAVIS WRIGHT

Rooted in Belonging:
Critical Place-Based Learning in Early Childhood and Elementary Teacher Education
MELISSA SHERFINSKI WITH SHARON HAYES

Transforming Early Years Policy in the U.S.:
A Call to Action
MARK K. NAGASAWA, LACEY PETERS, MARIANNE N. BLOCH, & BETH BLUE SWADENER, EDS.

Music Therapy With Preschool Children on the Autism Spectrum: Moments of Meeting
GEOFF BARNES

On Being and Well-Being in Infant/Toddler Care and Education: Life Stories From Baby Rooms
MARY BENSON MCMULLEN

Principals as Early Learning Leaders: Effectively Supporting Our Youngest Learners
JULIE NICHOLSON, HELEN MANIATES, SERENE YEE, THOMAS WILLIAMS JR., VERONICA UFOEGBUNE, & RAUL ERAZO-CHAVEZ

Resisting the Kinder-Race:
Restoring Joy to Early Learning
CHRISTOPHER P. BROWN

Reshaping Universal Preschool:
Critical Perspectives on Power and Policy
LUCINDA GRACE HEIMER & ANN ELIZABETH RAMMINGER, WITH KATHERINE K. DELANEY, SARAH GALANTER-GUZIEWSKI, LACEY PETERS, & KRISTIN WHYTE

Pre-K Stories: Playing with Authorship and Integrating Curriculum in Early Childhood
DANA FRANTZ BENTLEY & MARIANA SOUTO-MANNING

Ready or Not: Early Care and Education's Leadership Choices—12 Years Later, 2nd Ed.
STACIE G. GOFFIN & VALORA WASHINGTON

Teaching STEM in the Preschool Classroom:
Exploring Big Ideas with 3- to 5-Year-Olds
ALISSA A. LANGE, KIMBERLY BRENNEMAN, & HAGIT MANO

High-Quality Early Learning for a Changing World: What Educators Need to Know and Do
BEVERLY FALK

Guiding Principles for the New Early Childhood Professional: Building on Strength and Competence
VALORA WASHINGTON & BRENDA GADSON

Leading for Change in Early Care and Education: Cultivating Leadership from Within
ANNE L. DOUGLASS

For a complete list of series titles, visit https://www.tc ntinued

Early Childhood Education Series, *continued*

When Pre-K Comes to School: Policy, Partnerships, and the Early Childhood Education Workforce
BETHANY WILINSKI

Continuity in Children's Worlds: Choices and Consequences for Early Childhood Settings
MELISSA M. JOZWIAK, BETSY J. CAHILL, & RACHEL THEILHEIMER

The Early Intervention Guidebook for Families and Professionals, 2nd Ed.
BONNIE KEILTY

STEM Learning with Young Children
SHELLY COUNSELL ET AL.

Courageous Leadership in Early Childhood Education
SUSI LONG ET AL., EDS.

Teaching Kindergarten
JULIE DIAMOND ET AL., EDS.

The New Early Childhood Professional
VALORA WASHINGTON ET AL.

Teaching and Learning in a Diverse World, 4th Ed.
PATRICIA G. RAMSEY

In the Spirit of the Studio, 2nd Ed.
LELLA GANDINI ET AL., EDS.

Exploring Mathematics Through Play in the Early Childhood Classroom
AMY NOELLE PARKS

Becoming Young Thinkers
JUDY HARRIS HELM

The Early Years Matter
MARILOU HYSON & HEATHER BIGGAR TOMLINSON

Thinking Critically About Environments for Young Children
LISA P. KUH, ED.

Standing Up for Something Every Day
BEATRICE S. FENNIMORE

FirstSchool
SHARON RITCHIE & LAURA GUTMANN, EDS.

Early Childhood Education for a New Era
STACIE G. GOFFIN

Everyday Artists
DANA FRANTZ BENTLEY

Multicultural Teaching in the Early Childhood Classroom
MARIANA SOUTO-MANNING

Inclusion in the Early Childhood Classroom
SUSAN L. RECCHIA & YOON-JOO LEE

Moral Classrooms, Moral Children, 2nd Ed.
RHETA DEVRIES & BETTY ZAN

Defending Childhood
BEVERLY FALK, ED.

Starting with Their Strengths
DEBORAH C. LICKEY & DENISE J. POWERS

The Play's the Thing
ELIZABETH JONES & GRETCHEN REYNOLDS

Twelve Best Practices for Early Childhood Education
ANN LEWIN-BENHAM

Big Science for Growing Minds
JACQUELINE GRENNON BROOKS

What If All the Kids Are White? 2nd Ed.
LOUISE DERMAN-SPARKS & PATRICIA G. RAMSEY

Seen and Heard
ELLEN LYNN HALL & JENNIFER KOFKIN RUDKIN

Connecting Emergent Curriculum and Standards in the Early Childhood Classroom
SYDNEY L. SCHWARTZ & SHERRY M. COPELAND

Infants and Toddlers at Work
ANN LEWIN-BENHAM

Educating and Caring for Very Young Children, 2nd Ed.
DORIS BERGEN ET AL.

Beginning School
RICHARD M. CLIFFORD & GISELE M. CRAWFORD, EDS.

Emergent Curriculum in the Primary Classroom
CAROL ANNE WIEN, ED.

Enthusiastic and Engaged Learners
MARILOU HYSON

Powerful Children
ANN LEWIN-BENHAM

Supervision in Early Childhood Education, 3rd Ed.
JOSEPH J. CARUSO WITH M. TEMPLE FAWCETT

Guiding Children's Behavior
EILEEN S. FLICKER & JANET ANDRON HOFFMAN

The War Play Dilemma, 2nd Ed.
DIANE E. LEVIN & NANCY CARLSSON-PAIGE

Playing to Get Smart
ELIZABETH JONES & RENATTA M. COOPER

The Emotional Development of Young Children, 2nd Ed.
MARILOU HYSON

Young Children Continue to Reinvent Arithmetic—2nd Grade, 2nd Ed.
CONSTANCE KAMII

Bringing Learning to Life
LOUISE BOYD CADWELL

Bringing Reggio Emilia Home
LOUISE BOYD CADWELL

Pro-Blackness in Early Childhood Education

Diversifying Curriculum and Pedagogy in K–3 Classrooms

Gloria Swindler Boutte, Jarvais J. Jackson,
Saudah N. Collins, Janice R. Baines, Anthony
Broughton, and George Lee Johnson Jr.

Foreword by Joyce King

TEACHERS COLLEGE PRESS
TEACHERS COLLEGE | COLUMBIA UNIVERSITY
NEW YORK AND LONDON

Published by Teachers College Press,® 1234 Amsterdam Avenue, New York, NY 10027

Copyright © 2024 by Teachers College, Columbia University

All rights reserved. No part of this publication may be reproduced or transmitted in any form or by any means, electronic or mechanical, including photocopy, or any information storage and retrieval system, without permission from the publisher. For reprint permission and other subsidiary rights requests, please contact Teachers College Press, Rights Dept.: tcpressrights@tc.columbia.edu

Library of Congress Cataloging-in-Publication Data

Names: Boutte, Gloria, author.
Title: Pro-blackness in early childhood education : diversifying curriculum and pedagogy in K-3 classrooms / Gloria Swindler Boutte, Jarvais J. Jackson, Saudah N. Collins, Janice R. Baines, Anthony Broughton, and George Lee Johnson Jr. ; foreword by Joyce King.
Description: New York, NY : Teachers College Press, 2024. | Series: Early childhood education series | Includes bibliographical references and index. | Summary: "This book provides evidence-based curriculum examples, pedagogies, and resources; demonstrates how teachers can achieve Pro-Black teaching while also addressing curricular standards; and explains the benefit of Pro-Black teaching for all children"— Provided by publisher.
Identifiers: LCCN 2023043329 (print) | LCCN 2023043330 (ebook) | ISBN 9780807769140 (paperback) | ISBN 9780807769157 (hardcover) | ISBN 9780807782118 (ebook)
Subjects: LCSH: African American children—Education (Elementary) | African American children—Race identity. | Culturally relevant pedagogy—United States. | Education, Elementary—Curricula—United States.
Classification: LCC LC2771 .B68 2024 (print) | LCC LC2771 (ebook) | DDC 372.190973—dc23/eng/20231025
LC record available at https://lccn.loc.gov/2023043329
LC ebook record available at https://lccn.loc.gov/2023043330

ISBN 978-0-8077-6914-0 (paper)
ISBN 978-0-8077-6915-7 (hardcover)
ISBN 978-0-8077-8211-8 (ebook)

Printed on acid-free paper
Manufactured in the United States of America

Contents

Foreword *Joyce E. King* — vii

Prelude—"Pro-Black . . . Yes!" A Poem by Adrian Green — xiii

Introduction — 1
Gloria Swindler Boutte, Jarvais J. Jackson, Saudah N. Collins, Janice R. Baines, George Lee Johnson, and Anthony Broughton

1. Pro-Blackness in Early Childhood Education — 5
Gloria Swindler Boutte

2. Amplifying Pro-Black Perspectives in Child Development: The Children Will Be Well — 25
Anthony Broughton and Gloria Swindler Boutte

3. Drs. Diaspora Curriculum: Cultural Continuity From the Nile to the Niger to Rivers in the United States — 51
Gloria Swindler Boutte and George Lee Johnson

4. I'll Take You There: Envisioning and Sustaining African Diasporic Educational Spaces — 71
Jarvais J. Jackson

5. Africanizing the Early Childhood Curriculum: Exploring Pro-Blackness Through African Diaspora Literacy — 89
Saudah N. Collins

6. **Pro-Blackness as a Loving Antidote in Early Childhood Classrooms**   109
   Janice R. Baines

7. **African American Language (AAL): It's *the* Language for Me**   125
   Gloria Swindler Boutte

8. **What's Up, Fam (Family)?**   133
   Saudah N. Collins and Jarvais J. Jackson

9. **Reimagining Classroom "Management" Using Pro-Black and Restorative Approaches**   149
   Jarvais J. Jackson

Endnotes   173

References   175

Index   185

About the Authors   193

Foreword
In the Beginning There Was Blackness

Hey Black Child . . . /Do what you can do/And tomorrow your nation will be/What you want it to be

—from "Hey Black Child"
Useni Eugene Perkins, 1975

Useni Eugene Perkins wrote "Hey Black Child," the empowering literary classic in the Black Arts tradition in 1975 (Borelli, 2017). Brother Useni, a distinguished poet, playwright, sociologist, activist, and youth worker, was beloved in his hometown of Chicago, where he passed away on May 7, 2023, at the age of 90. I am honored to dedicate this brief foreword to Brother Useni's memory—to his literary accomplishments, his scholarship, and the courageous truth-telling legacy in defense of Black life, Black children's genius, and Black humanity that he captured poetically for eternity. "Hey Black Child" has inspired and nurtured the consciousness and identity of generations of our children—in classrooms where their teachers taught them to recite it and in Black families where their parents displayed the poem as an antidote to the undeniable "anti-Blackness" assaults even young children experience.

Brother Useni's African name means "tell me," or "testimony" in the language of the Chewa people of Nigeria. Imagine that. His father, Marion Perkins, a sculptor, and his mother, Eva, a domestic worker, boldly chose this prescient African name for their son in 1932. His parents named Useni's brother Toussaint—exemplifying and embracing the practice of African Diaspora literacy in Black family life nearly a century ago. I wonder if Brother Useni's playmates in the Ida B. Wells housing project where he grew up teased him about his African name, if his teachers claimed they couldn't pronounce "Useni"? What we do know is that his father, who was friends with the literary giants Richard Wright and Paul Robeson, exposed Useni to the arts at a young age. Indeed, Useni published his first poem in the *Chicago Tribune* at the age of 11.

It is this Black intellectual and communal tradition of academic and cultural excellence that this volume, *Pro-Blackness in Early Childhood Education*, demonstrates, offering us an empowering gift of courageous pedagogical truth-telling informed not only by Black scholarship but also by the authors' own culturally authentic Black family life experiences. Educators desperately need our expressions of cultural excellence demonstrated also in Adrian Green's poem, "Pro-Black . . . Yes!" that opens the volume. Educators need the Black scholarship referenced in this volume and the exemplary Black children's literature the authors include to illustrate Pro-Black pedagogy, both of which are too often missing in the education of teachers. And educators also need to know how to recognize and utilize the academic and cultural excellence practices of Black parents, elders, and our ancestors that the authors embody in their healing pedagogical practice.

ON ACADEMIC AND CULTURAL EXCELLENCE OR THE BLACKNESS OF BLACKNESS

Pro-Blackness can be understood as epistemology (liberating knowledge), ontology (African worldview and enduring values), and axiology (loving the beauty of Blackness) that is narrated in Black literature/orature, embodied in the academic and cultural excellence pedagogy of the Black teaching tradition (as well as the Black families' racial socialization practices), and scholarship in the Black liberation tradition that is about returning what we learn to the people (King, 2017)—all of which this volume demonstrates. Rather than recount and reify the ways in which Black children are victimized by anti-Black racism in education at all levels and society, the evidence of which is well-documented in extant research (Akua, 2023; Essien & Wood, 2023; Hale-Benson, 1990; and Van Ausdale & Feagin, 2001), the authors provide concrete examples of Pro-Black healing curriculum and pedagogy that can transcend these assaults and advocate *for* Blackness. Centering Blackness in this way means using our heritage knowledge and cultural traditions as resources for healing—from our communal practices in Black family life and Black literature/literacy to Black thought, advocacy, and community accountability (answerability) in research and scholarship (Patel, 2016). Indeed, Boutte notes that "the absence of Black literacy theories and Black-informed research are common omissions that contribute to anti-Blackness." This is definitely the case in early childhood teacher education (Wynter-Hoyte & Smith, 2020).

The healing lineage that this volume carries forward extends as far back as the legacies of Carter G. Woodson, W.E.B. Du Bois, and Frantz Fanon in the wider Black World. This lineage includes the contributions of Asa G. Hilliard, Barbara Sizemore, and Donald Smith, who have joined these ancestors. Baba Asa, Sizemore, and Smith were instrumental in advancing our understanding of academic and cultural excellence, with our beloved elder, Adelaide Sanford (2022). The National Alliance of Black School Educators (NABSE) issued a groundbreaking report, "Saving the African American Child," that articulated this important framing of educational excellence in 1983:

> Excellence in education is much more than a matter of high test scores on standardized minimum or advanced competency examinations. . . . Among other things, excellence in education must prepare a student for *self-knowledge* and to become a contributing problem-solving member of his or her own community and in the wider world as well. (NABSE, p. 11)

The four-pronged conceptual framework that Boutte and Johnson have developed in their Drs. Diaspora curriculum has certainly benefitted from this lineage, which also includes the foundational contributions of Amos Wilson, Na'im Akbar, A. Wade Boykin, Janice Hale-Benson, LaGarrett King, Gloria Ladson-Billings, our ally Ellen Swartz, and others whose scholarship is referenced in this volume. The scholarly lineage of academic and cultural excellence assembled in this volume stands in direct opposition to and as a bulwark against the current fascist political campaign across the United States that is banning books, whitewashing Black history curricula, and criminalizing teaching for Black solidarity, African diaspora literacy, and historical consciousness. We must recognize, however, that it is our peoplehood, and thus our humanity—our human right "to be African or not to be"—that is actually under assault (Hilliard, 2002; Nobles, 1997, 2023).

The contributing authors of *Pro-Blackness in Early Childhood Education* have demonstrated that they are unafraid and they are engaged in the fight back. We owe them a debt of gratitude for their vision, their perspicacity, and their courage. I am especially thankful for the way Gloria Boutte and her colleagues have embraced my work and advanced my thinking. The curriculum and pedagogy the authors present cogently and comprehensively in this volume and with such loving care are solidly rooted in Black humanity and fortified in Black spirituality—that is, in the humanizing practices of a "Pro-Black frame of reference." This volume demonstrates what educators need to know about this frame of reference, what they should be able to do and be like to understand and use the Black experience—and African diaspora literacy—as humanizing, healing pedagogy. This volume is a glimpse of the Pro-Black education future *for all children* that African diaspora literacy (that is to say, that the "Blackness of Blackness") offers us . . . and tomorrow our nation will be what we want it to be.

CODA

Ralph Ellison narrated this communal expression of the "Blackness of Blackness" in a Black church scene in his literary classic, *The Invisible Man. Pro Blackness in Early Childhood Education* can help us heed the message in this sermon (Ellison, 1952).

> "Brothers and sisters, my text this morning is the 'Blackness of Blackness.'"
> And a congregation of voices answered: "That blackness is most black, brother, most black . . ."
> "In the beginning . . ."
> "At the very start," they cried.
> ". . . there was blackness . . ."
> "Preach it . . ."
> ". . . and the sun . . ."
> "The sun, Lawd . . ."
> ". . . was bloody red . . ."
> "Red . . ."
> "Now black is . . ." the preacher shouted.

"Bloody . . ."
"I said black is . . ."
"Preach it, brother . . ."
". . . an' black ain't. . ."
"Red, Lawd, red: He said it's red!"
"Amen, brother. . ."
"Black will git you . . ."
"Yes, it will . . ."
". . . an' black won't . . ."
"Naw, it won't!"
"It do . . ."
"It do, Lawd . . ."
". . . an' it don't."
"Halleluiah . . ."
". . . It'll put you, glory, glory, Oh my Lawd, in the WHALE'S BELLY."
"Preach it, dear brother . . ."
". . . an' make you tempt . . ."
"Good God a-mighty!"
"Old Aunt Nelly!"
"Black will make you . . ."
"Black . . ."
". . . or black will un-make you."
"Ain't it the truth, Lawd?"

—Joyce E. King, PhD
Georgia State University

REFERENCES

Akua, C. (2023). *Dismantling the pre-school to prison pipeline through Black literacy and education transformation: Recommendations for school leaders, parents & policy makers* Wayfinder Foundation. https://www.wayfinder.foundation/resources.

Borelli, C. (2017, December 8). Useni Eugene Perkins may be the most famous Chicago poet you've never heard of. *Chicago Tribune.* https://www.chicagotribune.com/entertainment/ct-ent-useni-perkins-1208-story.html

Ellison, R. (1952). Prologue, *Invisible Man* (pp. 12–13)., Cited in H. L. Gates (1983). "The Blackness of Blackness": A critique of the sign and the signifying monkey. *Critical Inquiry*, 9(4), 720.

Essien, I., & Wood, J. L. (2023). "Treat them like human beings": Black children's experiences with racial microaggressions in early childhood education during COVID-19. *Early Childhood Education Journal.* https://doi.org/10.1007/s10643-023-01466-yWood

Hale-Benson, J. (1990). Visions for children: Educating black children in the context of their culture. In K. Lomotey (Ed.), *Going to school: The African-American experience* (pp. 209–222). State University of New York Press.

Hilliard, A. G., III (2002). *African power: Affirming African indigenous socialization in the face of the culture wars.* Makare.

King, J. E. (2017). Education research in the Black liberation tradition: Return what you learn to the people. *Journal of Negro Education, 86*(2), 95–114.

NABSE. (1983). *Saving the African American child: A report on the Task Force on Academic and Cultural Excellence.* https://blackcommunitycourse.files.wordpress.com/2013/01/savingtheafricanamericanchild.pdf

Nobles, W. W. (1997). To be African or not to be: The question of identity or authenticity—Some preliminary thoughts. In R. L. Jones (Ed.), *African American identity development: Theory, research, and intervention* (pp. 203–213). Cobb & Henry.

Nobles, W. W. (2023). *SKH: From Black psychology to the science of being.* Universal Write Publications.

Patel, L. (2016). *Decolonizing educational research: From ownership to answerability.* Routledge.

Perkins, U. E. (1975/2017). *Hey Black child.* LB Keys/Little, Brown and Company.

Sanford, A. (2022). *From enslavement to belovedness: For the dignity of my people.* Third World Press.

Van Ausdale, D., & Feagin, J. R. (2001). *The first R: How children learn race and racism.* Rowman & Littlefield.

Wynter-Hoyte, K., & Smith, M. (2020). "Hey, Black child. Do you know who you are?" Using African diaspora literacy to humanize Blackness in early childhood education. *Journal of Literacy Research, 52*(4), 406–431.

Prelude

"Pro-Black . . . Yes!"
A Poem by Adrian Green

*Pro-Black Nurturing . . .
. . . for a black boy or girl . . .

To counteract the nature!
. . . of a white world which negatively profiles from behind highly processed politically correct smiles . . .

Proactively protected, inoculated, immune boosted!
Prepared for a protracted dive deep into the darkest heart of whiteness . . .
(through a supremacist atmosphere even where there is not a single racist in sight)
Raised! to make sure dem laces laced tight!
Booted up and suited up . . . in the armor of pro-black consciousness . . .
. . . Inevitable anti-blackness preemptively contested,

    a black gloved fist,
    raised at the beginning of the race,
    before the starting gun goes off.

Pro-black starting blocks make the podium preordained when the finish line is crossed.
Early stage hard work creating thick skin while allowing the heart to stay soft,

    the head to stay high,
    the eyes to stay bright,
    the spirit to stay free,

---

*under pro-black tutelage . . .

under the weight of a society still predisposed to burdening the souls of black folk with heavy chains . . .

    . . . even if made of gold,
    or wrapped around brains . . .

Above-the-ground railroads lay tracks on the right side . . . towards change . . .

    . . . from early childhood . . .

. . . Full! Steam! Ahead! Fueled! by the renewable energy of history and heritage!
Launched! from the shoulders of giants!

Introduction

Gloria Swindler Boutte, Jarvais J. Jackson, Saudah N. Collins, Janice R. Baines, George Lee Johnson, and Anthony Broughton

We wrote this book against a backdrop of anti-Blackness in educational legislation and policies in the United States. Black histories are once again being maligned and marginalized. Notwithstanding, a key role that Early Childhood (EC) teachers should play in Black children's development is to help these children discover their purpose and how that purpose connects with the good of the community. We emphasize that Pro-Black pedagogies can serve as buffering and healing processes for Black children in the face of endemic anti-Blackness in society, educational settings, and the world.

Contrasting typical EC approaches that usually focus on the children on the individual level, Pro-Black pedagogies are communal and must necessarily be guided by the Black scholarship. Unlike commonly used child development practices that decenter children's racial identities, Pro-Black instruction builds on Black cultural dimensions (which are unpacked in Chapters 2 and 3). A key role of Pro-Black approaches is helping young children find out who they *be*. This habitual *be* (a nod to African American Language discussed in Chapter 7) connotes perpetuality—in the past, present, and future. To *be* in African thought is to (begin to, in the case of young children) understand one's destiny and a purpose.

Three pivotal life milestones are highlighted in African traditions: the day a person is born, the day they die, and the day they find out their purpose (a nod to Mark Twain for getting that right). So, holistic development from a Pro-Black stance includes ensuring children's cultural excellence (not just cognitive, social, physical, and emotional development). Indeed, cultural excellence is interrelated with other areas of development.

BOOK OVERVIEW

This book begins with a foreword from esteemed Pro-Black scholar Dr. Joyce King. She shares wisdom about Pro-Blackness in EC years.

After the foreword, we segue with a special treat, a poem, "Pro-Black . . . Yes!" by Barbadian poet Adrian Green. This sets the mood for the book.

Chapter 1 lays the foundation and provides an overview. We introduce key terms and explain what *Pro-Blackness* is and is not. We celebrate positive definitions of *Black*.

In Chapter 2, Anthony Broughton and Gloria Swindler Boutte emphasize that EC pedagogies should be guided by Black scholarship, which helps children find their authentic selves within the larger cultural context. Because of the dominance of Whiteness in "foundational" child development courses on theories and methods, it may be beyond readers' imagination to envision using a text like this one in EC teacher preparation courses instead of the contrite and overused (and sometimes use*less* when it comes to ensuring Black children's cultural and academic excellence) options. We think the time is right to require books like this one since Black perspectives in child development have been grossly underrepresented. We critique "foundational" theories by White males and offer Black scholarly thinking with the goal of helping Black children become powers for good.

Drs. Diaspora curriculum is shared in Chapter 3. This curriculum forms the basis of Pro-Black instruction highlighted in subsequent chapters. We emphasize two features at the center of the Drs. Diaspora curriculum: (1) focusing on cultural continuity and (2) using African diaspora literacies to teach African diaspora literacy.

Jarvais J. Jackson shares research on Saudah N. Collins's Pro-Black teaching using African diaspora literacy in Chapter 4. Clear examples are presented.

In Chapter 5, Saudah N. Collins speaks for herself and chronicles her development, thinking, and actions in African studies K–2 classes. She provides examples of resources and ideas for classroom décor and decorum.

To emphasize that Pro-Black teaching is not limited to African studies, Chapter 6 features EC educator Janice R. Baines. Janice provides examples of teaching in 1st and 2nd grades.

In Chapter 7, Gloria Swindler Boutte explains why and how AAL can and should be honored in Pro-Black classroom. Examples of children's books are offered.

In Chapter 8, Saudah N. Collins and Jarvais J. Jackson circle back to explain how Pro-Black family and community connections look. The first half of the book includes Saudah's philosophy, vision, and mission for including families. She presents examples and testimonials from families. She is intentional and involves families in-person and virtually. Jarvais's section complements the first half of the book by providing documentation from families about Saudah's engagement of their children as well as their thoughts about African studies.

We conclude the book with Chapter 9, written by Jarvais J. Jackson. Jarvais presents several Africancentric classroom community approaches such as Adinkra values, Ma'at, and nguzo saba. By embracing an Africancentric approach, EC teachers can embark on a journey towards equity, respect, and Pro-Blackness.

CHAPTER 1

Pro-Blackness in Early Childhood Education

Gloria Swindler Boutte

Your Blackness is safe here.
—Anthony Broughton (personal communication, 2022)

During a Fulbright-Hays project in Barbados focused on studying African American and Barbadian cultural connections, Rhonda Charles, a very wise natural health care practitioner, advised us to do three things to begin healing. She explained that we should pay attention to what we put in: (1) our bodies (e.g., diet and nutrition); (2) our thoughts; and (3) our environment. This sums up what Pro-Blackness is about. Loving Black children in Pro-Black ways is about ensuring that they are physically and psychologically safe and well. They should not be subjected to disrespectful treatment such as physical assault, invasive touching of their hair, and so on. They should be positively affirmed in their educational spaces with imagery, stories about them, and so forth. The environment should embrace them rather than exclude or negatively and inaccurately depict Black culture and history.

During the 20th-century Black Nationalist movement in the United States, we got a lot right. Pro-Blackness flourished in our bodies, minds, and environments. Children, youth, and adults could be heard chanting, "Black is beautiful!" Affirming songs like James Brown's "Say It Loud, I'm Black and I'm Proud" or Nina Simone and Aretha Franklin singing "Young, Gifted, and Black" filled the air. Natural hair styles and Black language flowed proudly. Black children were free to be themselves. The goal of this book is to facilitate healthy and positive development of Black children in ways that embrace their Black humanity and allow them to thrive. Pro-Blackness aims to create educational spaces where their Blackness is safe.

Figure 1.1. Carter Wearing *We Be Lovin' Black Children* Tee-Shirt

Recently, my daughter posted a photo of her son, Carter, proudly sporting his "We Be Lovin' Black Children" tee shirt on Facebook (Figure 1.1). In response, someone commented, "? . . . not all children?" (questioning if she *only* loved Black children).

The tee that Carter was wearing is a part of the Lovin' Black Children campaign launched to accompany the publication of *We Be Lovin' Black Children: Learning to Be Literate About the African Diaspora* (Boutte et al., 2021). The book is a clarion call for the unapologetic love of Black children in the face of endemic anti-Black racism in schools and society. *We Be Lovin' Black Children* is simultaneously an affirmation, a proclamation, a commitment, a promise, and an invitation to love Black children. The use of the African American Language (AAL) feature "habitual be" in the title connotes that we (authors and contributors) love Black children in the *past, present, and future—perpetually.* In the photo of Carter wearing the tee-shirt, it is clear to me that he feels loved and understands that Black children are beautiful, smart, and powerful. The love for Black children narrative is not widely conveyed in society and in schools.

I note that the affirmation "We be lovin' Black children" does not say "We ONLY love Black children." Likewise, the term "Pro-Black" does not mean anti-White or anti–other ethnic groups (Boutte et al., 2021 Herring et al., 1999; Wilson, 1978). It simply declares an unapologetic, positive, proactive perspective regarding Blackness and Black people and should not be misinterpreted to mean that scholars and educators focus *solely* on Black children (Boutte & Compton-Lilly, 2022). To make it plain, if I said I love purple, that does not mean that I dislike other colors or only love the color purple.

"We be lovin' Black children" means just that. To use a popular Black phrase, "we said what we said." We love Black children and refuse to stand by silently as their spirits, minds, and cultures are attacked. We present Pro-Black strategies for praxis (reflective action) in Early Childhood Educational settings. We hope you join us in this Pro-Black journey and mission.

A key goal of this book is to guide educators in creating spaces where Black children's humanity thrives. We know that there are many examples of *anti*-Blackness but intend to show what *Pro*-Blackness looks like in Early Childhood classrooms. *Pro* connotes *advocating for* Blackness; it does not mean going *against* anything else. The intensive focus on Pro-Blackness does not diminish or negate our concern about other racial groups, but we center Blackness in this book.

Though examples focus on U.S. contexts, we honor Black children everywhere. We also understand that there are many variations of Blackness, and that Black people live their Blackness in many complicated and sometimes contradictory ways (Boutte, 2022). That is, Black people are multidimensional and multispirited in our racial identities. Some may be apologetically Black; some may be African centered; and others may identify with double consciousness or another variation of Black identity. Sometimes, Blackness is nonexistent (assimilationist) or difficult to discern. As Howard noted (2010), "racial realities are so complex that no one set of experiences can serve as a representative reality for all individuals of a particular racial group" (p. 109). At the same time, common threads and deep structural cultural values exist—even when efforts have been made to eliminate and subjugate them. These intergenerational cultural dimensions should be included in the education of young Black children (Boykin, 1994; Hale-Benson, 1986; Hilliard, 1992; Wilson, 1978).

Pro-Blackness conveys *Black* in a positive manner. As beautifully demonstrated by King and Maïga (2018), Blackness, from an African epistemic framework, is positive. Dr. Maïga explains that in his Songhoy-senni language (spoken in Mali and other places in West Africa), *Blackness* is *only* viewed as positive. Consider the following examples:

- *Wayne bibi*—Black sun. When the sun is at its fullest expression at noon, the Songhoy people say, the sun is black.
- *Hari bibi*—Black water. When people are crossing the Niger River in a canoe and they want to drink clean, potable water, they ask for hari bibi, from the deepest part of the river.
- *Labu bibi*—Black earth. A Songhoy proverb says, "Do not plant your garden until the earth is black" (King & Maiga, 2018, p. 59).

While Blackness is positive from this African perspective, it is typically used negatively in English (e.g., "black sheep," "black eye," "blackball," "blackmail"). In the following sections, we share several endemic and persistent anti-Black societal and educational practices that make the focus on Pro-Blackness compelling and timely, especially during the foundational early childhood years. Endemic anti-Black attacks on Black children's language, culture, and histories are damaging to their spirits and souls. We recognize the power of *Black love* and offer Pro-Blackness as an educational process for healing.

ANTI-BLACKNESS IN EARLY CHILDHOOD EDUCATION SETTINGS

The blacker the berry, the sweeter the juice.

—folk saying

The timeless expression "The blacker the berry, the sweeter the juice" can be used to celebrate Blackness. The saying connotes that blackberries are sweeter once they turn black and ripen and is a metaphoric counternarrative for attacks on Blackness against the backdrop of endemic anti-Blackness. Yet I once heard someone add to the metaphor, "If it gets too Black, it ain't no use." I thought to myself, *we (Black folks) can't have nothin' without it being attacked;* anti-Blackness runs deep. When we say "Black lives matter," the counter is "White lives matter; Blue lives matter; *or* All lives matter." Seemingly, it never occurs that White lives matter *all the time* in the media, in law, in medicine, and in every institution—and, yes, in education. There is no need to declare love for White children as evidenced by their deep networks that are available in schools and society (e.g., Eurocentric curriculum, books, majority-White teachers, assessments, policies) (Earick, 2009). It would be grossly redundant.

People who vehemently disagree with the #BlackLivesMatter movement are silent around the reality that Black people are racially profiled. But the authors of this book *cannot* and will not be silent. We write this book to advance movement toward Pro-Black pedagogies and methodologies in Early Childhood Educational settings and in teacher preparation programs. We stand in solidarity with scholars and educators who are willing to step up, protect, and teach Black children like Carter via the engagement of critically conscious, Pro-Black strategies, curriculum, and instruction. We are speaking to those who are willing to *hear* and to actively disrupt anti-Blackness.

Pro-Black pedagogies and methodologies are important to Black children regardless of the setting (e.g., public, private, integrated, majority Black, majority White). It is equally important for children from all ethnic groups to learn about Pro-Blackness, lest they are socialized to effortlessly swallow and digest pervasive notions of anti-Blackness and continue the cycle of anti-Blackness as adults.

What Is Anti-Blackness?

Dumas and Ross (2016) named anti-Blackness as the most dominant form of racism in the United States. Anti-Blackness is defined as a particular *disdain* for Black people that is codified in U.S. laws, policies, and institutions. While I caution comparisons with the nature and type of racism experienced by other groups, I call attention to the reality that African Americans are the only racial group in the

United States who have been subjected to brutal, chattel enslavement for 246 years (10 generations). That distinction alone makes Black people's experiences in the United States incomparable (Boutte & Compton-Lilly, 2022).

We are all too familiar with the gross disproportionality among Black students in terms of special education placements, suspensions, and expulsions—with the highest percentage of suspensions for Black children at the preschool level (Gilliam, 2005). The omission of Pro-Black Early Childhood theories and pedagogies is complicit and problematic in anti-Blackness in teacher preparation programs. This book on Pro-Blackness in Early Childhood settings allows us to break the unhealthy silences regarding anti-Blackness that Black children experience in educational settings, albeit, sometimes not intentional on the part of the educators—though no less damaging.

While the focus of this book is primarily on U.S. contexts, we understand that anti-Blackness is experienced by African-descendant people on every continent. In recognition of this, the United Nations declared the years 2015–2024 as *the International Decade for People of African Descent.* Likewise, the #BlackLivesMatter movement in the United States calls attention to the need for justice and human rights for people of African descent.

For a brief moment in 2020, after the murder of George Floyd, people all over the world acknowledged the deeply ingrained anti-Black racism in the United States. For many educators from non-Black racial groups, this was a wake-up call regarding the need to interrupt anti-Black racism in educational contexts and to focus on Pro-Blackness. The Pro-Black movement was quickly displaced by national anti–critical race theory and anti–diversity, equity, and inclusion campaigns designed to create fear and confusion and continuation of White narcissism in schools. Many newly awakened educators, who had begun taking baby steps toward implementing Pro-Black pedagogies, quickly retreated, thus lapsing back into anti-Black teaching as a default. Black children continued to be dehumanized and mistaught. All this is to say that there is a longstanding history of anti-Blackness that is damaging to Black children. And it will not end until educators are intentional about making Pro-Blackness pervasive in K–12 educational settings and teacher educational programs.

Anecdotal Examples of the Impact of Anti-Blackness on Young Children

Anti-Blackness is so deep that young Black children often want to be any race other than Black. Though painful to think and write about, there are countless examples. Three exhibits are presented as follows. Two of the examples share comments by my grandchildren, who have been nurtured in an Africancentric home.

Exhibit 1

> When my granddaughter, Jaliyah, was 4 and attending a predominantly White preschool, she came home one day and announced that she wanted to be tan. As with my son, Jonathan (who actually wanted to be darker—see Boutte, 2008), I took the opportunity to talk with her about where we get our skin color. Of course, I discussed the beauty of brown and black skin. When I finished, Jaliyah said, "That is great, Dear,[1] but I still want to be tan! Tan! Tan! Tan!" She walked away. I chuckled to myself thinking of a preschooler's sense of finalism and knowing it all, but I was also sad because I realized that Jaliyah had figured out that there were privileges that went along with being lighter (tan was the color she called White people at the time). I intensified my African studies lessons with Jaliyah and Janiyah (Jaliyah's twin sister) and even took them to Kenya. . . . A few years later when Jaliyah was 6, she came to me one day and shared, "'Dear, remember when I wanted to be tan? Well, I do not anymore. I love being brown. And Black people have the best hair because we can do anything we want (to) with our hair."
>
> —Adapted from Boutte, 2017, pp. 250–251

Exhibit 2

> One day when riding in the car, Janiyah (who was 3 or 4 at the time) mused, "I hate brown. But I am brown so that must mean I hate myself." I was not sure what to make of these comments, but made mental notes to continue my home history lessons and affirmations.
>
> —Boutte, 2017, p. 252

Anti-Blackness can be internalized among children of other ethnic groups as well (e.g., Latinx, Asian).

Exhibit 3

> Most of my kindergarten students have already been picked up by their parents. Two children still sit on the mat in the cafeteria lobby, waiting. Occasionally, one of them stands to look through the door's opaque windows to see if they can make out a parent coming. Ernesto, the darkest child in my class, unexpectedly shares in Spanish, "Maestro, my mom is giving me pills to turn me White."'
>
> "Is that right?" I respond, also in Spanish. "And why do you want to be White?"
>
> "Because I don't like my color," he says.
>
> "I think your color is very beautiful and you are beautiful as well," I say. I try to conceal how his comment saddens and alarms me, because I want to encourage his sharing.
>
> "I don't like to be dark," he explains.
>
> His mother, who is slightly darker than him, walks in the door. Ernesto rushes to take her hand and leaves for home.
>
> —Segura-Mora, 2008, p. 3

I stress that these three examples are not isolated or random but are the result of systemic anti-Black racism. Even before the recognition of a racial pandemic in 2020, scholars alerted others to the need to proactively interrupt the ongoing, systematic assaults against Black children in educational settings (Boutte & Bryan, 2019; Givens, 2019; Johnson et al., 2017; Love, 2016). Boutte and Bryan (2019) focused specifically on five types of anti-Black violence in early childhood settings: (1) physical; (2) symbolic; (3) linguistic; (4) curricular and pedagogical; and (5) systemic school violence. We understand that these types of violence may be unintentional on the part of educators but acknowledge that damage to Black children's minds, bodies, souls, and education is still incurred. Anti-Black violence necessitates interruption and redirection via Pro-Black pedagogies and research. A description of each type of violence follows.

Physical violence. Physical violence refers to bodily assault on Black children such as hitting, pushing, and beating. It also refers to the residual health effects (e.g., high blood pressure, anxiety) of enduring ongoing anti-Black aggressions and discrimination. The effects of internal anxiety that Jaliyah, Janiyah, and Ernesto (in the previous three anecdotes) experienced may not be readily noticeable to adults, but childhood should not be burdened with worrying about skin color—a trait that they were divinely born with. Likewise, they should not be racially profiled because of their skin color.

Symbolic violence. Symbolic violence includes racial abuse, pain, and suffering against the spirit and humanity of Black children. It is realized in educational settings when educators misread Black children's culture, silence their voices, and reject their experiences and lived realities. Common examples include making disparaging remarks about Black children's names, hairstyles, and cultural ways of dressing. For example, Black children and their families often carefully select their clothing, paying close attention to detail—only to be mocked or punished for their cultural clothing choices.

Linguistic violence. Linguistic violence entails the marginalizing and policing of African American Language. Likewise, characterizing AAL as "broken English," "incorrect," or "not good" is linguistically violent. Privileging Standardized English and devaluing connections among language, race, and identity are also examples. Young children are very skilled at learning the language spoken by family members who care for them. A critique of their language not only fails to acknowledge the brilliance and humanity of being proficient with the language (e.g., AAL), it also simultaneously devalues family members who they learned the language from. The audacity of not recognizing the enormous feat of learning the language or the sophistication of AAL speaks to teacher preparation programs that have failed to teach prospective and inservice teachers about the beauty and complexity of African American Language. Sample strategies that honor AAL and build children's linguistic repertoires in Pro-Black ways will be discussed in Chapter 6.

Curricular and pedagogical violence. Curricular and pedagogical violence occurs when the curriculum is irrelevant, inaccurate, distorted, and incomplete. Sanitized and/or deficit-based versions of Black history are used instead of culturally informed ones. White children and children of color are presented with distorted mirrors of themselves in which Whiteness is presented as the prototype and Blackness as an anomaly or is omitted.

Pedagogical violence. Pedagogical violence is committed when educators unintentionally and/or intentionally minimize how teacher positionality shapes curricular decisions and instructional practices.

In teacher preparation programs and in professional development sessions, the absence of Black literacy theories and Black-informed research are common omissions that contribute to anti-Blackness. Chapter 2 includes examples of Black theories that are missing as well as curricular and instructional implications.

Systemic school violence. Systemic school violence is ingrained within educational structures, processes, discourses, customs, policies, and laws that often reflect anti-Black and hegemonic ideologies. Typical examples include the use of invalid assessments to measure Black students' language and achievement. The arrogance of thinking that it is good practice to use White theories to describe Black children's behavior becomes apparent if the situation were reversed. Most educators cannot imagine using measures normed on Black children to assess White children's development. Yet the opposite is routinely done with Black children as if they are acultural.

Given the anti-Black backdrop, it is clear why many Black children want to disassociate themselves with Blackness. Clearly, Eurocentric school and societal curricula are very effective—even among Black children in homes that are Africancentric like mine. The Early Childhood years are foundational and provide spaces where anti-Blackness can be interrupted and replaced with Pro-Blackness. Without Pro-Blackness, by the time children enter 4th grade, they will have been deeply doused in endemic anti-Blackness in schools and society. As June Jordan (1970) lamented, "for Black and Puerto Rican teenagers, school is almost a burial ground for joy and promise" (p. 95).

As evidenced in the previous discussion, little has changed since the 1970s. The good news is that despite the dismal anti-Black backdrop, there are examples of exemplary Pro-Black teaching. With Pro-Black pedagogies, this violence stops *now*. The authors of this book offer African diaspora literacy (ADL) as a healing pedagogical salve for anti-Blackness. We present a conceptual framework that explains four interconnected parts of ADL pedagogies and curriculum.

AFRICAN DIASPORA LITERACY: THE BLACKER THE BERRY, THE DEEPER THE ROOTS

For the past two decades, I have been engaged in ongoing engagement with a cadre of K–12 teachers, doctoral students, and faculty to better understand how Pro-Blackness looks in classroom settings and teacher education programs. For this book, we focus on Early Childhood years, but readers should know that the work can be and has been extrapolated across K–12 school settings, teacher preparation programs, and professional development for teachers.

African diaspora literacy is presented as a concrete pedagogy for actualizing Pro-Blackness in educational settings. The concept is derived from Dr. Joyce King's (1992) definition of *diaspora literacy*. Drawing from Busia's (1989) work, King defined diaspora literacy as Black people's knowledge of their (collective) story and cultural dispossession. In 2017, I added the word *African* to the phrase to make explicit the focus on African-descendant people and epistemologies (Boutte et al., 2017). Dr. Joyce King, my mentor, welcomed the addition and currently uses the term. Simply put, African diaspora literacy means being literate about Black people's histories, cultures, epistemologies, axiologies, ontologies, and so forth (Boutte et al., 2021). Being literate about the African diaspora enables us to collectively address commonly faced, persistent, and pervasive issues.

ADL relates to African-descendant people wherever they are in the world (e.g., Africa, U.S., Caribbean, Brazil, Europe). The assumption is that people in the African diaspora have informed and indigenous perspectives that lead to self-recognition, healing, and "re-membering" (King, 1992). Re-membering is "a process for recovering history by putting back together the multiple and shared knowledge bases and experiences that shaped the past" (King & Swartz, 2014, p. xiii). King (personal communication, September 27, 2014) explained that African people should strive for ADL "in order to recover our heritage from ideological knowledge, distortions, and omissions but also so that we can relate to and be useful in the liberation struggle here (U.S.) and on the continent." Yet Black children, and other children, are currently deprived of this important knowledge base and dispositions. This pervasive process of anti-Africanism is so endemic that it frequently is unnoticed even among scholars in Africa and people in the African diaspora (Boutte et al., 2017). This trend has resulted in multigenerational illiteracy on African diasporic knowledge and collective inaction, in many cases.

African diaspora literacy is beneficial to people of African and non-African descent and can result in deeper understandings of ways African worldviews help "disrupt Eurocentric hegemonic paradigms that depend on oppression and hierarchy in opposition to justice and human freedom" (Ladson-Billings, 2018, p. xiii). ADL scholars assume that people can not only learn *about* African diasporic culture and perspectives, they can also learn *from* them as well. New ADL scholarship has the potential to positively impact educational practices and policies that rarely adequately and accurately address the worldviews of people in the African diaspora (Boutte et al., 2021; Jackson et al., 2021; Johnson et al., 2018).

Framework for African Diaspora Literacy Pedagogies and Methodologies

While ADL pedagogies and methodologies are not prescriptive, four constituent and interrelated components of ADL can be seen in pedagogies, theories, and methodologies (see Figure 1.2):

1. Black historical consciousness themes (King, 2020);
2. African values and principles (Jackson et al., 2021; King & Swartz, 2016);
3. Black cultural dimensions (Boutte, 2016; 2022; Boykin, 1994); and
4. Historical and contemporary perspectives (Boutte, 2016; 2022).

There is no specific order for these four components, but all are needed for ADL pedagogies and methodologies. Each component will be briefly mentioned here, but clarifying examples will be presented throughout this book.

Figure 1.2. Interlocking Components of African Diaspora Literacy

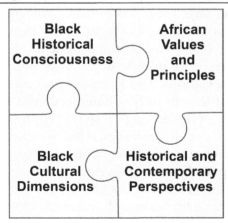

Black historical consciousness themes. Black historical consciousness themes include a focus on Africa and the African diaspora; the role of power and oppression; Black agency, resistance, and perseverance; Black joy; Black identities; and Black historical contention (King, 2020). These themes are recursive and integrated throughout the year. In Table 1.1, I expound on how King's (2020) Black historical consciousness themes can be applied in Early Childhood settings.

Table 1.1. Black Historical Consciousness Principles and Classroom Ideas

Themes/ Possible Topics	Commentary and Implications for Young Children	Classroom Ideas
1. Power and Oppression	Even young children understand power dynamics, whether it is in their home with adult roles or in school with teachers and peers, so these experiences can be used as grounds for dialogue about racial groups. Exhibits 1, 2, and 3 on pp. 11–12 demonstrate that young children are thinking about issues of race and color. As early as age 2, children use race to reason about people's behaviors, apply color names to skin color, and begin asking questions about their own racial identities (Derman-Sparks & Edwards, 2010). Hence, Early Childhood educators have an opportunity to engage them in critically conscious conversations about anti-Blackness and Pro-Blackness.	• Recognize racial identity as a specific area of development. • Engage children in regular informed conversations about race. • Children can examine classroom library selections and count how many books are about Black people and can decide what to do about it. • Children can write or draw dialogue poems or pictures (Boutte, 2022) in which they divide the paper into two sections and brainstorm about two perspectives on the same topic. Teachers can start by putting two fairy tales in conversation with each other (e.g., "The Three Little Pigs" and "The True Story of the Three Little Pigs" (Scieszka & Smith, 1991). Conversations can move to how people within families can hold different perspectives about issues. Scieszka, J., & Smith, L. (1991). *The true story of the little pigs: by A. Wolf.* Puffin, • Make a conscious effort to share books, movies, music, and other texts that demonstrate injustices, inequalities, and inequities that Black people experienced throughout history.

(continued)

Table 1.1. (continued)

Themes/ Possible Topics	Commentary and Implications for Young Children	Classroom Ideas
	Silence about race reinforces racism since children will draw conclusions based on what they see without guidance and mediation from critically conscious adults.	• Below are a few sample texts[1] that feature young children in the storyline that can be used to open and deepen conversations about anti-Black racism and ways to fight against it: » Coleman, E. (1996). *White socks only*. Albert Whitman & Company. » Coles, R. (1995). *The story of Ruby Bridges*. Scholastic. » Johnson, A. (2007). *A sweet smell of roses*. Simon & Schuster Books for Young Readers. » Wiles, D. (2005). *Freedom summer*. Aladdin. » Woodson, J. (2001). *The other side*. Nancy Paulsen Books. A resource for positive Black books is Mahogany Books, which can be found online at https://www.mahoganybooks.com/children/.
2. Black Agency, Resistance, and Perseverance	Children need to learn that throughout history—from ancient Africa to present day—Black people have exerted their agency and resistance and persevered against anti-Blackness.	A compelling way to begin this discussion is by listening to music (e.g., spirituals, freedom songs in the United States and throughout the African diaspora; African resistance songs such as "Something Inside So Strong" by Labi Siffre). "Something Inside So Strong" is a theme song of the Children's Defense Fund Freedom Schools, and videos of children performing it make for a great start (e.g., do an Internet search for the YouTube video from AIC Freedom School at https://www.youtube.com/watch?v=HaxvKxzKkxE). Sample Texts • Cline-Ransome, L. (2013). *Light in the darkness. A story about how slaves learned in secret*. Jump At the Sun Publishers.

(continued)

Table 1.1. (*continued*)

Themes/ Possible Topics	Commentary and Implications for Young Children	Classroom Ideas
		• Hannah-Jones, N., & Watson, R. (2021). *The 1619 project: Born on the water.* Penguin. • Myers, S. L. (2015). *New shoes.* Holiday House.
3. Africa and the African Diaspora	All children of color, but especially Black children, need to learn and hear often that the history of their ancestors did not begin with enslavement and contact with White people (Boutte, 2016; 2022; King, 2020; Woodson, 1933/1990). Indeed, historians have documented thousands of years of history of African people *before* slavery. And as brutal and horrific as it was, the 246 years of chattel slavery represents a brief period of time in the existence of African people. Over time, young children will come to understand that White people and culture are not prototypes for Black children's lives, nor are Black children dark-skinned versions of White children.	Teachers can aim to demonstrate African legacies across time and space. A few sample books are below. • Chocolate, D. (1996). *Kente colors.* Walker and Company. • Diouf, S. A. (2000). *Kings and queens of West Africa.* Scholastic. • Ellis, V. F. (1989). *Afro-bets first book About Africa.* Just Us Books. • McDermott, G. (1987). *Anansi the spider: A tale from the Ashanti.* Henry Holt & Company • Medearis, A. S. (1994). *Our people.* Gingham Dog Press. • Musgrove, M. (1976). *Ashanti to Zulu: African traditions.* Penguin. • Musgrove, M. (2001). *The spider weaver: A legend of Kente cloth.* Scholastic. • Nebthet, K. N. (2015). *Light as a feather: 42 laws of MAAT for children.* Ra Sekhl Arts Temple. • Ofori, I. E., & Ofori, B. (2020). *Princess Akoto: The story of the golden stool and the Ashanti kingdom.* Tellwell Talent. • Onyefulu, I. (1996). *Ogbo: Sharing life in an African village.* Gulliver Books.

(*continued*)

Table 1.1. *(continued)*

Themes/ Possible Topics	Commentary and Implications for Young Children	Classroom Ideas
4. Black Joy	Black joy is African-descendant people's experiences and expressions of life that are not focused on hardship. Joy is needed to sustain people's spirits (King, 2020). Like other humans, Black people's lives include love, collegiality, collectiveness, and happiness. Teachers need to be intentional in showing Black joy without trivializing it. King (2020) offered several topics that can be included: Black family, music, dance, expression, cuisine, the arts, literature, popular culture, sports, and so forth.	Invite Black families, children, and educators to show, write, and draw what Black joy looks like in their lives, historically and presently. This is particularly important against the backdrop of the abundance of Black suffering that is a key part of the school narrative. Share songs like "Say it Loud, I'm Black and I'm Proud" (James Brown) or "Young, Gifted, and Black" (Aretha Franklin and/or Nina Simone). Examples of books showing Black joy: • Lyons, K. S. (2019). *Going down home with Daddy*. Peachtree. • Mattox, C. W. (1989). *Shake it to the one that you love the best: Play songs and lullabies from Black musical traditions*. Warren-Mattox Productions. • Milner, D. (2017). *Crown: An ode to the fresh cut*. Agate Bolden. • Pinkney, B. (1997). *Max found two sticks*. Aladdin Paperbacks. • Tarpley, N., & Lewis, E. B. (1998). *I love my hair!* Little, Brown.
5. Black Identities	Black people perform their racial identities in a multitude of ways. A key part of the Early Childhood years from a Black perspective is for young children to deliberate on their divine purpose. Presenting a variety of options will be helpful in terms of pointing children toward their interests.	Educators should be intentional about providing more complete, diverse, and equitable depictions of Black people (e.g., different socioeconomic statuses; gender orientations; geographic locales; generations; languages; abilities) across time and space. Sample texts • Byers, G. (2018). *I am enough*. Balzer & Bray. • Cook, M. (2009). *Our children can soar: A celebration of Rosa, Barack, and the pioneers of change*. Bloomsbury.

(continued)

Table 1.1. (*continued*)

Themes/ Possible Topics	Commentary and Implications for Young Children	Classroom Ideas
		• Holman, S. L. (1998). *Grandpa, is everything Black bad?* Culture Co Op. • Nyong'o, L. (2019). *Sulwe*. Simon & Schuster Books for Young Readers. • Perkins, U. E. (2019). *Hey Black child*. LB Kids. • Pippins, A. (2020). *Who will you be?* Wade Books. • Wyeth, S. D. (2002). *Something beautiful*. Dragonfly Books.
6. Black Historical Contention	Including Black historical contention (debatable and/or complex points) reminds us that since there is variation among Black people in terms of their identities, they may disagree on some issues. This allows us to present Black people as complex individuals (King, 2020). When we present a complete picture of Black history, it does not have to be romanticized where Black people are only depicted as virtuous. Since all humans have virtues and vices, we need to be mindful of how these have played out historically and contemporarily. Young children can certainly understand this as family members and friends demonstrate a range of virtue and vice within and among themselves.	Engage children in critical literacy where they examine issues such as how women were subjugated during the Black nationalist/civil rights movement, in science, math, and so on. A caveat is that since most of Black history has focused only on minute, inaccurate, and distorted portrayals of Black people and culture, there is a vast need for positive counternarratives. Be sure to complicate the picture and discuss contentions, but do not overdo it. Dialogue poems, pictures, and stories can be used to demonstrate that two things can be true at the same time, though seemingly at odds (Boutte, 2016; 2022). This shows the complexity and infallibility of humans—all humans, not just Black people.

(*continued*)

Table 1.1. (continued)

Themes/ Possible Topics	Commentary and Implications for Young Children	Classroom Ideas
	An example is the first Black U.S. president, Barack Obama, whom many/most African Americans view as a hero. Yet other African Americans critique his lack of action on issues related to Black people. That said, his significance as the first Black president rightly remains, though contested by some. This example shows that people have virtues and vices and also that there is variation in the ideologies and beliefs of Black people.	

African values and principles. African values and principles include focusing on African ontology, epistemology, axiology, principles, and virtues. These values and principles undergird the lives of African people globally (King & Swartz, 2014; 2016). In several chapters of this book, we make it explicit how we teach young children about enduring African values and principles using Adinkra symbols.

Black cultural dimensions. Black cultural dimensions include aspects of Black culture that have been documented worldwide among African people: spirituality, harmony, movement, verve, affect, communalism, expressive individualism, oral tradition, social time perspective, perseverance, and improvisation (see Boutte, 2022; Boutte et al., 2017; Boykin, 1994; Hale-Benson, 1986; Hilliard, 1992; King, 2005; and King & Swartz, 2014, 2016; for a more complete description of each dimension). While culture morphs over time, deep cultural structure remains, though it manifests itself differently depending on the context and time. These cultural dimensions will be highlighted throughout the book and described in Chapter 2.

Historical and contemporary perspectives. The aim is to research and teach about continuities of Africanism across time and place. The goal is to show African humanity and culture on a continuum. As emphasized by Dr. Carter G. Woodson (1933/1990), the education of a people should start with the people themselves, so all research, teaching, and service will begin with Africa and African perspectives.

In this book, we demonstrate how these four ADL components can be integrated throughout lessons, units, projects, and activities in Early Childhood educational settings.

EXTRAPOLATING AFRICAN DIASPORA LITERACY

I am not African because I was born in Africa but because Africa was born in me.

—Kwame Nkrumah

The authors of this book are Africanists who love everything about African ways of being—good, bad, and ugly. I quickly note that this is not a requirement for teachers or teacher educators, though we invite readers to start their own journeys to develop African diaspora literacy. We have continuously developed knowledge bases and experiences to position ourselves on this ongoing, Pro-Black journey using ADL to guide our teaching. This book is a great start for those who want to develop African diaspora literacy, but the journey is continuous. We emphasize that all racial groups are invited to develop ADL and, indeed, hope that this book provides an inspiration to do so.

The other authors and I have been able to extrapolate African diaspora literacy work in our respective spaces. In this book, readers will witness the four-pronged conceptual framework (Black historical consciousness, Black cultural legacies, historical and contemporary perspectives, and African values and principles) come alive in Early Childhood classrooms and theories.

ADL work is getting traction as is evidenced by the two awards with the co-edited volumes (Boutte et al., 2021; Johnson et al., 2018). These all demonstrate our deep love for Black children everywhere and Pro-Black stances that will sustain them and allow them to flourish.

CHAPTER 2

Amplifying Pro-Black Perspectives in Child Development
The Children Will Be Well

Anthony Broughton and Gloria Swindler Boutte

I hear what you're saying about this theory and stuff, but I feel like these theories don't speak to the real experiences of Black children. Yesterday while my cousins were playing, . . . they created a game called "Superhero Hide and Seek" with his neighbors. Before the game started, each of the five children—three African American boys, two White boys—selected a superhero character. Superman, Spiderman, Iron Man, and Ninja Turtle were selected. When it was my cousin's turn, he said, "I'm the Black Panther, 'cause I'm Black!" I was shocked first that he included that he was Black, but even more shocked that he relinquished his role as an avid Spiderman fan, to become the "Black Panther." At 6 years old, race was prominent in his pretend play. No offense, but how do these theories address this?

—Broughton, 2022, p. 23, adapted with permission

All over the world, African worldviews and epistemologies have been and are currently being overlooked, undervalued, and delegitimized.

—Boutte et al., 2017, p. 66

Early Childhood Educators in the United States enter their classrooms armed with theoretical knowledge bases as tools for analyzing and understanding the children they teach. The theories are almost exclusively developed by European men (or European American in the case of Dewey) whose studies only reflect White middle-class norms and perspectives (Lewis & Taylor, 2019; Wilson & Peterson, 2006). To seal the indoctrination of the perceived importance and legitimacy of Whiteness and male influence in the Early Childhood Education (ECE) profession, standardized tests like the PRAXIS (Educational Testing Services [ETS], 2019) reinforce these theories as a part of the certification process. Test takers are evaluated on their knowledge of "the major contributions of foundational theorists to education" and the ability to relate "the work of theorists to education contexts: Bandura, Bruner, Dewey, Piaget, Vygotsky, Kohlberg, and Bloom" (ETS, 2019, p. 6). Contextually, these "foundational" theories are based on studies that were not conducted in the United States. They exclude Black (and other) perspectives and thus reify systemic racism. Given this framing of what counts as official knowledge and *who* can be a theorist, Black scholars have been excluded. If European theories are the only ones that educators are required to draw from, it is no surprise that Black children continue to be culturally assaulted, misdiagnosed, labeled, miseducated, mistreated, misunderstood, marginalized, and psychologically murdered as they are learning while Black (Boutte & Bryan, 2021; Hale, 2001; Love, 2016).

The endemic (covert and overt) atrocities Black children encounter in the educational settings compelled Boutte (2016; 2022) to ask educators, "How are the (Black) children?" (Boutte, 2016; 2022). This question was inspired by a traditional greeting of Masai warriors of Kenya. Legend has it that the Masai were considered among the most accomplished and fabled tribes in Africa, with warriors who were both fearsome and intelligent. They would greet each other with "Kasserian ingera," a traditional greeting that means, "And how are the children?" The anticipated response was "The children are well," to confirm a state of peace and safety, ensuring the safety of the young and powerless.

Across time and space, Black children are not well in educational spaces and society at large (Boutte, 2016; 2022; Boutte & Bryan, 2021; Ladson-Billings, 2022; Love, 2019). In *The Souls of Black Folk,* W. E. B. Du Bois (1903) lamented that Black people are often asked (indirectly), "How does it feel to be a problem?" Black children have been, and continue to be, positioned as a problem in educational spaces where they should feel safe. Rather than subscribing to deficit paradigms that do not address the needs of

Black children, we draw from Pro-Black knowledge bases and educational scholars and share approaches for cultivating the genius in Black children.

We understand Black children's holistic wellness as mutually beneficial to children, families, educators, and society at large. We invite Early Childhood educators to use Pro-Black pedagogies to ensure that Black children thrive in educational spaces. A key principle of this book is that **Pro-Black pedagogies must necessarily be guided by the scholarship of Black scholars.** We suggest that these knowledge bases are instructive for learning not only *about* Black scholarship but *from* it as well. We acknowledge that Black theories and scholarship are not the cure-all or a panacea, but note their importance to understanding inside perspectives about Black children's development. Using instructional practices informed by Black scholarship is one way educators can begin to heal and buffer Black children from anti-Blackness. Thus, for Pro-Black pedagogies, Black informed practices are essential.

AMPLIFYING PRO-BLACK PERSPECTIVES IN CHILD DEVELOPMENT

We amplify insights from the works of Dr. Amos Wilson, Dr. Janice Hale-Benson, Dr. Asa Hilliard, Dr. Barbara Bowman, Dr. Na'im Akbar, and Dr. Alfred Wade Boykin to honor the contributions of Black educational scholars. These are likely to be unfamiliar names for many ECE educators, regardless of their racial backgrounds, since these scholars' work is typically not included in any substantive way in teacher preparation programs. Hence, we amplify the urgency of applying Pro-Black child educational theories in ECE classrooms. Pro-Blackness is presented as a strategy for decolonizing classrooms and disrupting mainstream deficit interpretations of Black children (Broughton, 2020).

Honoring the South African philosophy *ubuntu* (I am because we are) and embracing collectivism, we interconnect and apply Pro-Black perspectives and concepts about Black children from Black scholars. We do this as an act of resistance against the Western philosophy of individualism, which dominates society. In the spirit of ubuntu, the contributions of these Black scholars are synthesized (consistent with collectivism), rather than highlighting their contributions as individuals only.

Dr. Alfred Wade Boykin's (1983) groundbreaking scholarship documented 11 African American cultural dimensions:

1. spirituality;
2. harmony;
3. movement;
4. verve;
5. affect;
6. communalism/collectivity;
7. expressive collectivism;
8. oral tradition;
9. social time perspective;
10. perseverance; and
11. improvisation.

These essential deep cultural dimensions have been documented by other scholars (e.g., Boutte, 2016; 2022; Boutte et al., 2021; Hale-Benson, 1986; Hilliard, 1992, 2002; Johnson et al, 2018a; Shade, 1997). While Black culture is dynamic and manifests itself in different ways over time and space, these 11 dimensions and others (such as rhythm) are intergenerational cultural legacies that Black children need to thrive. These indelible cultural legacies are redemptive and reparatory for Black children, yet they are absent in most European theories. We use these intergenerational cultural legacies (dimensions) to organize our discussion of Pro-Black theories. We note that the dimensions overlap and are interrelated and should be thought of likewise instead of as discrete categories.

We have documented the existence of these dimensions in our scholarship by studying connections among Black people in the diaspora. Collectively, we have documented these 11 cultural dimensions on every continent except Antarctica. For example, we have examined connections between African American and African/Caribbean cultures (Barbadian, Cameroonian, Ghanaian, Jamaican, Nigerian, Sierra Leonean, and South African) through funded grants (Fulbright-Hays, Fulbright Scholar, Fulbright Specialist, and Spencer Foundation).

In Table 2.1, we note ways that these 11 cultural dimensions show up in Black scholarship and demonstrate how they

Table 2.1. Black Cultural Dimensions and ECE Theories

African American Cultural Dimensions	Representation in Black ECE Scholarship	Bandura (Represented in theory)	Bruner (Represented in theory)	Dewey (Represented in theory)	Piaget (Represented in theory)	Vygotsky (Represented in theory)	Kohlberg (Represented in theory)	Bloom (Represented in theory)
1. Spirituality—as an approach to life, places emphasis on vitality rather than mechanism, believing that nonmaterial forces influence human events.	Boykin (1983) Hilliard (1991) Wilson (1978)	No	No	No	No	Yes	Yes	No
2. Harmony—refers to the interconnectedness of one's way of life with other elements in the scheme of things, so that humankind and nature work in harmony.	Boykin (1983) Hilliard (1991)	No	No	No	No	No	No	No
3. Movement—a core component of psychological health, which integrates movement, rhythm, percussiveness, music, and dance.	Boykin (1983) Hale-Benson (1986) Hilliard (1991) Wilson (1978)	No	No	Yes	No	No	No	No

(*continued*)

Table 2.1. (continued)

African American Cultural Dimensions	Representation in Black ECE Scholarship	Bandura (Represented in theory)	Bruner (Represented in theory)	Dewey (Represented in theory)	Piaget (Represented in theory)	Vygotsky (Represented in theory)	Kohlberg (Represented in theory)	Bloom (Represented in theory)
4. Verve—the ability to stimulate relatively high levels of activity and to express energy and vibrancy in action.	Boykin (1983) Hale-Benson (1986) Hilliard (1991) Wilson (1978)	No	No	Yes	No	No	No	No
5. Affect—emphasizes emotions and feelings along with a sensitivity to emotional cues and a tendency to express emotions.	Boykin (1983) Hale-Benson (1986) Hilliard (1991) Clark & Clark (1947) Wilson (1978)	No	No	No	No	No	No	No
6. Communalism/collectivity—develops social connectedness, which entails a recognition that each individual has responsibilities and social ties that go beyond themselves as individuals.	Boykin (1983) Hale-Benson (1986) Hilliard (1991)	Yes	No	Yes	No	Yes	No	No

7. Expressive individualism—encompasses the development of a distinct personality and the tendency to express oneself spontaneously and authentically.	Boykin (1983) Hale-Benson (1986)	No	No	Yes	No	No	No
8. Oral tradition—emphasizes the capabilities of oral and aural communication, in which both speaking and listening are viewed as performances, as well as cultivating oral virtuosity. Spoken language that is alliterative, metaphorically colorful, and graphic in nature.	Boykin (1983) Hale-Benson (1986) Hilliard (1991) Wilson (1978)	No	No	No	No	No	No

(*continued*)

Table 2.1. (*continued*)

African American Cultural Dimensions	Representation in Black ECE Scholarship	Bandura (Represented in theory)	Bruner (Represented in theory)	Dewey (Represented in theory)	Piaget (Represented in theory)	Vygotsky (Represented in theory)	Kohlberg (Represented in theory)	Bloom (Represented in theory)
9. Social time perspective—a perspective in which time is viewed as passing through a social space rather than a material space, and as recurring, personal, and phenomenological. It also implies that time is subjective and that it is constantly changing, depending on the context and the individual's perspective. The concept of time is acknowledged as a social construct.	Boykin (1983)	No	No	No	No	No	No	No

32

10. Perseverance—embodies an attitude of resilience and determination that gives a person the courage to keep going, even when the odds seem stacked against them.	Boykin (1983) Hale-Benson (1986) Hilliard (1991)	No	No	No	No	Yes	Yes	No
11. Improvisation—alternatives are substituted for those more sensitive to Black culture. This allows Black people to reclaim their cultural identity and create a safe space where they are respected and appreciated.	Boykin (1983) Wilson (1978)	No	No	No	No	No	No	No

33

are missing in most of the "foundational" ECE (Bandura, Bruner, Dewey, Piaget, Vygotsky, Kohlberg, and Bloom). We also present classroom examples of Pro-Black pedagogies using Black cultural dimensions.

Each of Boykin's (1983) 11 African American cultural dimensions can be applied in classrooms to provide holistic support for Black children. Here we share examples of how four of the Black cultural dimensions (spirituality, communalism, verve, and affect) might be used in classrooms with young children.

Spirituality

> Seven-year-old Kwame tearfully enters the classroom and embraces his teacher, Mr. Jenkins. Kwame cried, "'Big Mama' (grandmother) passed." Sharing his condolences, Mr. Jenkins said, "I'm here for you." Kwame said, "My mama told me to pray if I get sad. She said my grandma went to heaven." Kneeling to Kwame's eye level, Mr. Jenkins consoled, "If you need some time, go to the safe place and take as much time as you need."

Mr. Jenkins understood that spirituality is and has been a source of strength for Black people. He made accommodations by providing social and emotional support to Kwame during his bereavement. Mr. Jenkins understood that Kwame could not isolate his spirituality from his identity as a student and that he (Kwame) could not perform well academically in the midst of spiritual trauma. Mr. Jenkins's response aligned with Hilliard's (1995) Pro-Black perspective of education, which embraces education as a vehicle to cultivate the mind, body, and soul of a child. In African tradition, the role of the teacher is to appeal to the intellect, humanity, and spiritual needs of the students, because the body is viewed as a divine temple that houses the spirit. Spirituality is a key facet of African American personality and culture that should not be overlooked or dismissed (Boykin, 1983). Asa Hilliard (1995) suggested that to truly cultivate the mind, body, and spirit of children, teachers must first recognize and believe that Black children have a divine purpose and destiny. As a result, they can see, speak, and teach to each child's *intellect, humanity*, and *spirit*, which will support children in experiencing transformation to their best selves, which is only done in concert with the community.

That is, each person has their own unique destiny, but that destiny is interdependent with the community.

From a Pro-Black perspective, teachers can cultivate children's spirit and character using traditional/indigenous African values, such as the ancient principles of Ma'at (Delpit & White-Bradley, 2003; Hilliard, 1995; Wilson, 1978). In contrast to the Lady Justice, an American symbol (which is said to be inspired by Themis, the Greek goddess who represented law, order, and justice), Ma'at predates Themis. She existed in ancient Egypt (Kemet) before Themis (and carried a sword and feather of truth). Ma'at was more than just a goddess; she was an embodiment of truth, justice, righteousness, order, reciprocity, harmony, and balance, which was Kemet's society's model for order, morality, and balance.

In Table 2.1, we acknowledge that Kohlberg's theory focuses on moral development. We also note that his conception of moral development is not quite the same thing as spirituality from a Black perspective. From an African spiritual perspective, all humans are born into goodness. This point in itself stands in contrast with Western views of people being born in sin. What this means for educators is that they should always seek to find the good in the children they teach—even when it is challenging to do so. Black children, like all children, are in the process of learning what it means to be a member of their respective communities. The goal is to help them figure out their divine purpose.

As feminist critiques have pointed out, Kohlberg's research privileged White men and suggested that they were more likely to reach the "higher" stages of moral development. Teachers may miss the opportunity to nurture Black children's spirit if they draw solely from Kohlberg's theory of moral development, which follows a universal invariant sequence of stages towards the same universal ethical principles in all cultural settings. Kohlberg (1971) stated, "Almost all individuals in all cultures use the same thirty basic moral categories, concepts, or principles; and all individuals in all cultures go through the same order or sequences of gross stages of development" (p. 176). Kohlberg's higher stages emphasize equality and individual autonomy, while Africancentric spirituality is immensely communal in nature. The responsibility that individuals have to the community as a part of their divine purpose is at the core of Pro-Black perspectives on moral maturity.

Spirituality emphasizes the power of the individual through the source of a higher being to shape their own. From a Black perspective, spirituality also connects individuals to other humans as a part of our divine, collective purposes. Mr. Jenkins understood the importance of the moral support offered through the joint embrace. As Hale-Benson (1986) highlighted in her research-based program for preschool children (Visions for Children), frequent touching, lap-sitting, holding hands, and hugging are encouraged to support Black children's affect (a related Black cultural dimension). This recommendation stands in stark contrast to the "hands-off" approaches in ECE spaces currently.

In Black culture, sharing grief is important to healing. Teachers can provide children with a quiet space to pray or meditate. Children should be engaged in conversations about respecting time in the quiet space, as they may be engaged in sacred practices. Teachers can also demonstrate sensitivity to children's spirituality by being intentional about how holidays are handled in the classroom. Families can be engaged via dialogue or a short survey to find out what holidays they celebrate. Teachers can allow students to discuss special days during morning meetings or sharing times. It is likely that holidays that are typically omitted in schools but celebrated at home will emerge in these conversations (e.g., King Holiday, Juneteenth, Kwanzaa).

Teachers should also reflect on ways their spirituality influences and shapes their classroom approaches and interactions with children and their families. We know that spirituality is connected to students' cognitive, emotional, physical, and social development in complex ways. Teachers can also support students in their spiritual development through the usage of African proverbs. Hale-Benson (1986) found that the integration of African proverbs in the curriculum supported children in accessing folk wisdom, life skills, and models of resilience. For instance, the West African version of the folktale "The Tortoise and the Hare" (Nuurali, 2022) can be used in tandem with the discussion of everyday activities as well as with stories of local and national Black figures to teach children about perseverance. Teachers can plan lessons and critical thinking activities around books like *African Proverbs for All Ages* by Johnnetta Betsch Cole (2021). Children can make meaning of the proverbs and engage in interactive writing activities with the teacher as they reflect on life lessons and concepts they can apply to their lives. And of course, Black children can gain much insight from the perennial stories about Anansi the spider. Indeed, proverbs play an integral role in the spiritual development of Black people and should be routinely integrated into ECE lessons.

Although Lev Vygotsky conceptualized human development as a socially mediated process of children acquiring cultural values, beliefs, and problem-solving strategies through collaborative dialogues with a more knowledgeable other (MKO), he does not provide examples from an African context. For instance, a Western perspective would consider an MKO to be someone who simply possesses more knowledge than another person, but an MKO in the African tradition carries a deeper meaning, as a highly revered, generational expert with indispensable wisdom used to cultivate and sustain the mind, body, and souls of African people. It can be implied through Vygotsky's sociocultural theory that children's cognition is shaped by their sociocultural context, but his theory offers no specific moral guidance for application from a Pro-Black context. This limitation manifests in our vignette with Mr. Jenkins and Kwame, where Mr. Jenkins's guidance from Vygotsky's theory would have likely been limited to offering cognitive or linguistic guidance to support Kwame. On the other hand, insights of Pro-Black scholars like Boykin (1983), Hale-Benson (1986), and Hilliard (1995) provide Mr. Jenkins with rich, indigenous support to recognize, embrace, and respond to mental, physical, and *spiritual* needs of Kwame, rather than solely his mind (academics).

Spirituality from a Pro-Black frame of reference connects the individual to the extended family or society. Life pathways and purposes are dependent on relationships with others. Black children have a tacit understanding of communal connectivity, and the focus on individualism is often at odds with spiritual expectations of Black culture.

Pro-Black Activities to Support Spirituality

1. Consider playing a variety of music for typical ECE activities. Include Black genres such as spirituals, jazz, rhythm and blues[1] (Hale-Benson, 1986).
2. Share books that teach children about truth, balance, order, harmony, propriety, and reciprocity as they figure out their

(spiritual) purpose in life. Nebthet, K. N. (2015). *Light as a feather: 42 laws of MAAT for children*. Ra Sekhl Arts Temple.

Communalism

When Gloria's grandson, Carter, was 3 years old, he walked into her living room and saw a book showcasing a contemporary Thai living room decor on display (think cover of Architectural Digest *or* Better Homes and Gardens *that showcases beautiful rooms). Studying the book cover, he asked, "Where are the people?"* (personal communication, July 13, 2014).

In this anecdotal account, Carter was disoriented by a picture of a room with no people. His life is filled with people all around—an extended family comprised of six people in the home—most in constant motion. His existing conception (schemata) of home does not fit the sterile picture of the living room on the cover of the book. In his understanding of home, people are more important than things like furniture.

This example also helps us understand the complexities of culture. As a member of Black culture, Gloria immediately understood Carter's query, "Where are the people?" To borrow from Luther Vandross, "A house is not a home."

Though both Carter and Gloria share Black culture, Gloria's life experiences have resulted in a wider repertoire of the concept of home. As a part of her deep cultural experiences, both people and the decor are central to home. For Carter, the thing that makes a house a home is the people. Young children are busy figuring out many possibilities of being human. In educational settings, they often do not see mirrors and affirmations that match their cultural conceptions of life.

Three months later, Carter saw the book being displayed again and asked, "Where are the people?" (personal communication, October 25, 2014). Over time, as he learns about cultures outside his own, he will likely view the Thai example as yet another manifestation of humanity that is valuable while not detracting from his own. Given what we know about Black children's spiritual development and relation to other areas of development (e.g., emotional), a few activities are suggested.

By now, it is more than evident that spirituality is closely related to communalism from an African perspective. Communalism entails a recognition that each individual has responsibilities and social ties that go beyond themselves as individuals. A communal ethos centers collectivity over individualism. This collectivity is essential to meeting one's life goals.

Three of the "foundational" ECE theorists in Table 2.1 have a focus on some aspects of communalism (Bruner, Dewey, and Vygotsky). For example, while Jerome Bruner's theory does not explicitly address communalism, certain aspects of his ideas can be related to communal values and practices. His emphasis on social interaction, culture, and language, as well as constructivist learning principles, may be viewed as being supportive of the communal approach to children's cognitive development. Likewise, Vygotsky's theory focuses on sociocultural development, learning, and the role of social interactions in cognitive development. Dewey's theory comes closest to capturing the centrality of communalism in educational success. His notions of collective decision-making and problem-solving align with communalism from an Africancentric perspective. Like the Black cultural dimension of communalism, Dewey's theory promotes interconnectedness, social consciousness, and community solidarity as can be seen in the works of Boykin (1983), Hale-Benson (1986), and Hilliard (1991). As evident in the multiple examples in Chapter 5 (Saudah N. Collins—K–2nd grade) and Chapter 6 (Janice R. Baines—1st and 2nd grade), the creation and sustainability of communal spaces in ECE classrooms should be organic rather than perfunctory.

Pro-Black Activities to Support Communalism

1. Engage children in communal activities and games such as hand-clap games where groups of children can join in.
2. Unity circles (class meetings and discussions) should be held daily so children can share things in their community or topics that they are interested in. This helps develop a communal space as relationships among children are deepened through discussions of the similar and different experiences that they bring.

Verve

"Funga Alafiya, Ase Ase! Funga Alafiya, Ase Ase," the preschool children's voices rang out as they sang a well-known West African welcome song. As the children danced along with the YouTube video, showing their best moves, their voices were strong and rhythmic.

Each morning, their teacher, Ms. Love, plays Pro-Black songs like this as children enter the classroom and engage in freestyle dancing and singing.

Laughter and joy fill the air as the students prepare for their unity circle discussion about things of interest to them.

Tacitly or intentionally, Ms. Love's use of energetic songs and movement is undergirded by the understanding that African American learning style originates from a harmonious, expressive, musically inclined, and movement-oriented culture (Boykin, 1983). Verve encompasses intense energy that manifests itself through expressive body language or other stylistic ways of communicating. People with high verve levels value a stimulating and lively environment. It is the combination of both physical and mental energy that innately supports many Black children in performing tasks with enthusiasm and drive. It can be achieved through activities such as music and movement. Misunderstanding verve has contributed to teachers making erroneous assumptions about Black children (Hale-Benson, 1982). Children with high levels of verve are often misperceived as disengaged, off task, have poor attention spans, lack organizational skills, and exhibit passive-aggressive behaviors (Boykin, 2001). Consequently, in many cases children are expelled, suspended, or referred to special education (Vasquez, 2005). The children are not the issue. Teachers should pause, reflect, and evaluate if their classrooms are responsive to Black cultural dimensions or if children are being punished for simply exhibiting key aspects of their humanity.

When education professionals fail to conceptualize the cultural context of children's behavior through an indigenous lens (Hilliard, 1995; Wright & Counsell, 2018), they run the risk of misinterpreting, mislabeling (Eide & Eide, 2006; Levy, 2018), and inappropriately disciplining (Noguera, 2008). This contributes to a national crisis, namely the preschool-to-prison pipeline, by which the melanin of Black children is weaponized and used to stigmatize and criminalize them (Adamu & Hogan, 2015; Gilliam, 2005; Noguera, 2008; Wright & Counsell, 2018). While some teachers claim that Black children are troublemakers (Boutte, 2016; Wright & Counsell, 2018), culturally relevant educators depict them as brilliant and gifted (Boutte, 2016; Hale-Benson, 1986; Ladson-Billings, 2022; Paris, 2012; Wright & Counsell, 2018).

Boykin (1978; 1983) recommended that educators engage children in problem-solving and hands-on activities to stimulate verve, which resulted in Black children performing better cognitively. Boykin and Cunningham (2001) found that African American children require vervistic pedagogical methods to learn effectively in school, yet most schools remain culturally relevant to White Americans by using mundane, non-energetic instructional activities.

Teachers can incorporate methods such as role-playing and interactive simulations or investigations to engage children. Black scholars like Amos Wilson (1992) and Hale-Benson (1982) cautioned teachers against confining children for long periods of time and suggested that children be provided with maximum opportunities for movement and exploration. Both scholars found that stimulating, supportive, and patient teachers cultivated high-achieving students. A balance between quiet and active learning activities that encourages children to move while they are learning is recommended (Hale-Benson, 1986).

Although some early childhood scholars receive credit for their innovative, stimulating, and engaging instructional approaches, Webber (1978) chronicled the work of a Black nursery teacher who was enslaved to demonstrate innovative educational approaches on the plantations.

> Aunt Dinah . . . ran her nursery like the kindergarten of today. [Her] inventive brain kept the children always busy. She told stories, demonstrated how animals could be made from potatoes, orange thorns, and a few feathers, and helped her pupils set table with mats made of the green leaves of the jonquil, cups and saucers of acorns, dishes of hickory hulls and any gay bit of hila they could find. . . . She also helped them dress up as flowers and taught them to make decorations with chains of china blossoms and long strings of chinquapin. (p. 15)

Although she was not deemed a theorist, Aunt Dinah knew the power of child engagement. She knew that she had to keep the children busy with innovative and meaningful activities. From kingdoms like Kush to the pyramids of Ancient Kemet, to plantations, Black people across the African diaspora have always demonstrated effective pedagogical acumen that teachers can draw from (see, e.g., *The Kongo Art of Babysitting* (Fu-Kiau & Lukondo-Wamba, 1988)).

In Table 2.1, we note that Dewey's theory readily lends itself to verve in classrooms. He stressed the importance of active learning in classrooms. Here we find congruence with several overlapping Black cultural dimensions such as verve, communalism, movement, and affect.

Pro-Black Activities to Support Verve

1. Children can be provided instruments like African drums, balafons, and shekeres[2] to create their own songs to reinforce content.
2. Engage children in African hand-clap games such as Miss Mary Mack.
3. Engage children in a variety of stimulating music like educational rap songs and African/Caribbean music.
4. Teachers should engage with children and show interest by moving, dancing, and interacting with them, rather than being observant.

Harmony

> While playing outside, a group of preschoolers in MISTER B's[3] class noticed that there was trash on their playground. A few children recalled and mentioned a lesson about taking care of the environment and how a person's decisions (e.g., littering) can impact the lives of others (i.e., trash on the playground in the children's playspace). Creating raps and call-and-response is customary in MISTER B's class, and one of the preschoolers, Tyron, began to chant verses from one of the songs, "Clean up! It's time to clean up." MISTER B responded, "Work as a team to get the job done." After cleaning the playground, the children gathered around MISTER B to discuss how we all must work together in harmony to keep our environment clean.

In MISTER B's classroom, he stressed ways that humans are connected to each other and to nature. The concept of harmony or interdependence/oneness of being enables an understanding of self that transcends history, absolute time, and the physical body's limitations (Akbar, 2003; Hilliard, 1995; Nobles, 1976). Teachers who draw from Pro-Black knowledge bases understand that a child's community/village and connection to their ancestry is essential to their identity and self-concept. From an African context, self-definition is defined by one's people rather than by individuality alone. Teachers can begin cultivating harmony in their classrooms by fostering collective learning, rather than independent, competitive environments.

The interpersonal interactions of Black children with their family have accustomed them to learning collectively, rather than solely in isolation (Hale-Benson, 1982). The development of thematic lessons can also support children in conceptualizing the idea of interconnectedness with nature. For instance, when teaching children about plants, the teacher can contextualize the lesson with local farmers in the community and show how African indigenous knowledge about farming informs their practices. Teachers can also teach respect and appreciation through harmony, by sharing that if farmers did not grow crops, we would not have food to eat. This underscores the concept of ubuntu.

When Africans were kidnapped during the European slave trade, they were so ingenious that they braided seeds into their hair so that they would have access to food wherever they ended up. Virtually all content areas that children learn can be traced back to Africa (e.g., science, math).

Harmony can also be fostered through classroom design and climate. Hale-Benson (1982) described harmonious classrooms as those that are aesthetically appealing to children. She suggested that classrooms reflect homelike features like couches, rocking chairs, and nature elements. Teachers can also cultivate harmonious environments by incorporating images or artwork that reflect the community and cultural values of Black children, like pictures of family and community members, Black leaders, and Adinkra symbols or hieroglyphics. Cultivating harmonious classrooms can support Black children in experiencing a sense of belonging because they know that they are valued and loved by their teachers. Harmonious environment also supports Black children who tend to be more people oriented, feeling oriented, and proficient at nonverbal communication (Hale-Benson, 1982), by providing these children a sense of safety to express themselves. It is also essential that teachers maintain a clean and organized classroom, free from disorganization, clutter, and inconsistency to support children with mental clarity and stability.

Pro-Black Activities to Support Harmony

1. Connect students to nature via outside activities like gardening.
2. Share stories about Black people who were known for working in concert with nature (e.g., George Washington Carver).
3. Share examples of Black people's agency during enslavement when they organized escape plans using signs from nature (e.g., springtime, northern directions, paying attention to birds migrating).
4. Find examples of harmony from families and community members.

Affect

> While riding home from school, 5-year-old Courtney told her father that her teacher did not like Nareo (a Black male). When her father asked why she thought that, Courtney explained, "Because she always puts him in time out. If anything is broken, she calls his name first."

Even as a young child, Courtney is reading emotional signals of the adults and children around her. Affect is an emphasis on emotions and feelings together with a special sensitivity to emotional cues and a tendency to be emotionally expressive (Boykin, 1978). From a Pro-Black perspective, there is not a dichotomy between emotion and intellect, and young Black children develop an astute ability to think about emotions and to feel them as well. Indeed, like most areas of development, there is a complex interplay between emotion and intellect.

While social and emotional learning (SEL) has received considerable attention in recent years, most SEL curriculums do not consider race or the ways systemic racism affects and influences children's social–emotional development. Though anti-Blackness is endemic in schools and society (Dumas & Ross, 2016), little to no consideration is given to Black children's lived experiences of being exposed to social inequities in a racialized society. Black children are especially vulnerable to messages of White superiority and Black-degrading behavior (Boutte et al., 2021b; Wright et al., 2022). Black children's cultural expressions are continuously policed in terms of their hairstyles, dress, body language, or movement (Wright et al., 2022). Theories regarding child growth and development are incomplete without acknowledging the role race plays and has played in the lives of Black people across the African diaspora (Muller et al., 2022). We cannot fully cultivate the social–emotional learning of Black children without acknowledging that "race-centered violence kills Black children on a daily basis by either murdering them in the streets—taking their bodies or murdering their spirits—taking their souls" (Love, 2016, p. 6). Unfortunately, Black children are more likely to be exposed to police violence, racial profiling by law enforcement officers, and unwarranted attention by police to their caregivers, even if the children themselves are not the victims of these police practices (Love, 2016). Such exposure increases the likelihood of children suffering from toxic stress. In the midst of the "smog" (Tatum, 2007, p. 65) of racism that our children are forced to breathe in order to survive, we must cultivate within them African self-concept development (the extended self) to help them thrive (Love, 2019).

Many Black children are not afforded opportunities to freely express themselves in ways that affirm and inspire them (Broughton, 2016). In fact, many of them learn through emotional cues and microaggressions early on that they would have to "act" in ways perceived to be White in order to be seen, heard, validated, and accepted as intelligent. Understanding the roles of systems of oppression in shaping social identities, Boutte (2016), Hale-Benson (1982), Hilliard (1995), Akbar (2003), and Boykin & Toms (1985) all contended that the development of positive self-identity should be an integral aspect of the education of Black children. Black children experience double consciousness, which consists of conflicts between how they feel inside and how the world perceives them (Du Bois, 1903; Fanon, 1952; 1963) and how they express it.

Play observations can offer teachers a glimpse into children's identity and affect development (Broughton, 2016; Wilson, 1978). Wilson

(1978) coined the term *schizoid play*, in which Black children grapple with double consciousness by imitating characters and images that do not reflect their own. It is important to note that we do not accept the term "schizoid" as an internal mental disorder but as a reaction to a sociocultural circumstance that the child has been placed in (Broughton, 2016). Instead of "schizoid play," Broughton (2022) recommended the term, "Double Conscious play." Double Conscious play occurs when a child's experience grappling with the conflict of how they feel inside and how the world perceives them manifests itself through play (Broughton, 2022). Similarly, Hale-Benson (1986) described this phenomenon as a "duality of socialization" (p. 62). When Black children realize that the heroic or imitable images in their imagination cannot reflect their cultural identity, which limits them from truly expressing themselves through this role, they become frustrated and experience what Wilson (1978) referred to as "frustrated play."

Oppression and social identity development play a major role in shaping Black children's affect. Black social psychologists Kenneth and Mamie Phipps Clark (1947) examined children's attitudes toward race and skin tone and challenged the Supreme Court's "separate but equal" concept of public schools (Plessy v. Ferguson, 1896) with their scholarship. Based on Clark and Clark's (1947) study, racism negatively impacted the development of children's self-concept. This study continues to be relevant since children still form, experience, and express positive and negative biases about themselves and others (Long et al., 2018). CNN (2010) reported that some children develop racist views as early as preschool (Derman-Sparks & Ramsey, 2006; Long et al., 2018). To develop self-concept while cultivating positive affect, children must see their own voice, ethnicity, and the ethnicities of others as beautiful. Hale-Benson (1986) called this "self-concept development." None of the "foundational" theories address this Black cultural dimension in ways that capture Black children's emotional intelligence as evidenced by their ability to read complex and covert racial innuendos and to make sense of it all as they develop.

Pro-Black Activities to Support Affect

1. Children can be provided opportunities to express themselves through visual arts. They can use art materials to express their emotions, thoughts, and perspectives.

2. Children can express themselves through poetry, song, hip-hop, movement, dance, or other stylistic interpretations and performances.
3. Teachers can encourage conversations by being present and in the moment by showing children uninterrupted, genuine interest when children are speaking. Teachers can extend children's conversations by asking follow-up questions and encouraging children to share their thoughts without judgment.

BLACK THEORIES FOR BLACK CHILDREN

The previous examples about the centrality of Black cultural dimensions can be instructive as Early Childhood (EC) teachers reflect on the way forward. Although we highlighted four of the 11 Black cultural dimensions, all are important. An important takeaway is that theoretical guidance should be informed by the thinking of Black scholars. Black scholarship draws from intergenerational cultural legacies and strength that are important for Black children's cultural and academic excellence. As Wade Boykin (1994) wrote, "African American children are not tabula rasas and they certainly are not simply inadequate dark skinned white children" (p. 250). Indeed, it is quite audacious to think that theories about White children should be unquestionably applied to Black children's development. This does not imply that some aspects of the so-called foundational theories *may* not be useful in some cases. Pro-Black educators understand that reflection on Black children's sociocultural realities is necessary for excellent teaching. Likewise, the realization that ECE spaces and curricula are not neutral and are teeming with Eurocentrism, which no doubt feels very comfortable for White children and very damaging to Black children.

Black children are constantly told they are insufficient and incapable of learning implicitly or explicitly (Boutte, 2016; Broughton, 2019; Emdin, 2016). As children mature, they become aware of how their intellect is perceived, and they internalize those perceptions as well. Unfortunately, many educators believe that Black children are insufficient and incapable of learning because of the deficit theories they have been indoctrinated to embrace during their teacher preparation process. Amos Wilson (1978) cites the omission of theories about Black early childhood as the greatest failure of U.S. developmental, educational, and clinical psychology. The use of IQ tests to wrongly prove that Black people were intellectually inferior was supported by prominent educational figures like Edward Thorndike and G. Stanley Hall (Hilliard, 1995; Woodson, 1933). Education professionals still rely on intelligence and other standardized tests to measure children's learning and proficiency, despite their racist history and present. Researchers and culturally responsive educators have noted the flawed nature of standardized tests and warn that children know more than standardized tests can capture (Ladson-Billings, 2017; Long et al., 2018). Educators can explore and embrace Boykin's (1994) Afrocentric cultural/relational cognitive styles model to support students in demonstrating intelligence through other mediums, such as the performing arts (Boutte, 2016).

Most certified teachers in the United States are formally trained and evaluated (ETS, 2019) on their ability to apply "foundational" educational theories on all children to justify instructional decisions (Wilson & Peterson, 2006). These theories have influenced universalistic understandings of children's learning and development in ECE spaces (Broughton, 2022; Lewis & Taylor, 2019; Wilson & Peterson, 2006). U.S. teachers' historical adherence to the "foundational" educational theorists (ETS, 2019) has contributed to a foundation of White privilege, which has not worked favorably for Black children. That is in part because teachers and educational policy makers continue to apply White theories to Black skin (Broughton, 2022). There is an African proverb that says, "Until the lion tells his side of the story, the tale of the hunt will always glorify the hunter." Here we have called for the narratives and theories of Black scholars to be integrated into ECE settings.

CONCLUSION

I (Gloria) recall how Black theories and scholarship were marginalized in my early career in the 1980s and 1990s. I eagerly waited for an occasional special issue of the *Child Development* journal to read articles by a few Black scholars. Because of narrow definitions of what constituted research, Black scholars knew that

Black-focused scholarship was unlikely to be published in this so-called top-tier journal unless it was a *special issue*. Our work and thoughts were treated as if they were peripheral and not important. Likewise, the Black scholarship about Black children's development has been overlooked. If we are serious about educating African American children in ways informed by Black scholarship, we first have to stop glorifying all things European. We must draw from the wisdom from African-descendant scholars and engage in Pro-Black pedagogies.

CHAPTER 3

Drs. Diaspora Curriculum
Cultural Continuity From the Nile to the Niger to Rivers in the United States

Gloria Swindler Boutte and George Lee Johnson

> *It's the doctors. (yeah yeah). It's the doctors. (ooooh) It's the doctors (doctors)—the African Diaspora.*
> *Ancient Africa (talkin' 'bout)*
> *Enslavement (talkin' 'bout)*
> *Reconstruction (talkin' 'bout)*
> *Jim Crow (talkin' 'bout)*
> *Soon I will be done with the troubles of the world.*
> *Civil Rights (talkin' 'bout)*
> *Black Nationalism (talkin' 'bout)*
> *African Americans*
> *We shall overcome some day.*
> *How 'bout the children? (talkin' 'bout)*
> *We be talkin' 'bout. We be talkin' 'bout.*
> *How 'bout the children? (talkin' 'bout)*
> *Soon I will be done with the troubles of the world.*
> *How 'bout the children? (talkin' 'bout)*
> *How 'bout the children? (talkin' 'bout)*
> *It's the doctors! The African Diaspora! (echo Diaspora Diaspora)*

These lyrics to the one-minute Drs. Diaspora theme song are the first thing that children hear when we serve as historians in resident in schools. It was created by William Boyles, a teacher for the Center for the Education and Equity of African American Students (CEEAAS). The song gives an overview of what Drs. Diaspora curriculum is about. After hearing the song, we see if anyone knows the meaning of *diaspora*. Thus far, no one has, so we do a little activity where we gather all of the children in the center of the room.

On the count of three, we ask them to spread out (disperse) and go to another chosen spot in the classroom. While they are there, we ask them if they are the same person as they were in their previous spot(s). We ask:

- Do you still speak the same language(s)?
- Do you still have the same family members?
- Are you still wearing the same clothes and so forth?

We conclude that in essence, they are the same person, but they have relocated to different places in the room. We explain that many African people were dispersed (spread out) across the world, but that they brought their culture with them. We clarify that as Drs. Diaspora, we will teach them about African people and culture around the world (in the diaspora). On the count of three, all children return to their original spots.

OVERVIEW OF DRS. DIASPORA CURRICULUM

Drs. Diaspora is a 4-to-8-week curriculum that focuses on the historical and contemporary culture, history, and language of people in the African diaspora. We are the creators—two PhDs (Dr. Gloria Swindler Boutte and Dr. George Lee Johnson) who are both Africanists. We are a "pair of docs" who teach about the African diaspora; thus the name *Drs. Diaspora.*

Both of us are nationally and internationally known scholars who have published and taught about the African diaspora for decades. As noted in Chapter 1, this is certainly not a requirement for educators, but we share our positionality to illuminate our expertise for creating a curriculum. As readers will note in subsequent chapters written by some (of many) of our academic legacies (Janice R. Baines, Anthony Broughton, Saudah N. Collins, and Jarvais J. Jackson), our goal is to expand African diaspora literacy and Pro-Blackness. To this end, we invite readers to join in this important journey and mission of teaching about the African diaspora as this content is grossly undertaught in schools.

Both of us have visited, taught in, presented, and/or lived in places where African-descendant people are the majority (see Table 3.1).

Table 3.1. Places Visited Where Majority of People Are African Descendant

Locale	Context	Year(s)
Ghana, West Africa	(Gloria)—Member of a Fulbright-Hays Group Abroad project studying connections between African American and Ghanaian culture. Focused on European slave trade. 4 weeks	2003
Ghana, West Africa	(Gloria)—Study Tour. Focused on Ghanaian culture. 2 weeks	2003
Choco, Quibdo Colombia, South America	(Gloria) Visiting Scholar. University of Technology at Choco. 2 weeks	2007
Sierra Leone, West Africa	(Gloria). Led (with Susi Long) Fulbright-Hays Group Abroad project studying connections between African Americans in the Sea Islands and Sierra Leonean culture and language. (George—member of team). 4 weeks	2011
South Africa, Zambia, and Botswana	(Gloria and George). Study Tour. 2 weeks	2012
Jamaica	(Gloria) Visiting Scholar. University of West Indies. (George—Study Tour). 2 weeks	2013
South Africa	(Gloria). Visiting Scholar. Stellenbosch University. (George—Study Tour). 2 weeks	2013
Nigeria	(Gloria). Fulbright Scholar. (George) Visiting Scholar—Taught at the University of Uyo. 2 semesters	2015–2016
Guyana, South America	(Gloria) Visiting Scholar. University of Guyana. (George—Study Tour). 2 weeks	2017
Cameroon, Central Africa	(Gloria). Led (with Gwenda Greene) Fulbright-Hays Group Abroad project studying connections between African American Language and Kamtok (George—member of team). 4 weeks	2017
Egypt (Kemet)	(Gloria and George). Study Tour with Anthony Browder. 10 days	2018
Ghana, West Africa	(Gloria). Led (with Gwenda Greene) a Fulbright-Hays Group Abroad project studying connections between African American Language and Kru takk. (George—member of team). 4 weeks	2018

(continued)

Table 3.1. (*continued*)

Locale	Context	Year(s)
Nigeria, West Africa	(Gloria and George). Led (with Gwenda Greene) a Fulbright-Hays Group Abroad project studying connections between African Americans and Yoruba culture, spirituality, and language. 4 weeks	2022
Barbados	(Gloria and George). Led (with Gwenda Greene and Tondaleya Jackson) a Fulbright-Hays Group Abroad project studying connections between African Americans in the South Carolina and Bajan culture and language. 4 weeks	2023
Ghana	(Gloria and George). Led inaugural *Drs. Diaspora* Ancestors' Tour to reconnect African Americans with their African culture. 10 days	2023

Our continuous goal is to learn about African-descendant people's culture wherever they are in the world. While in these African diasporic spaces, we position ourselves as learners and integrate what we learn into the Drs. Diaspora curriculum. We look for examples of Black cultural dimensions across time and space.

We present the Drs. Diaspora curriculum as complementary to ongoing Pro-Black instruction. It is generative and adaptive, depending on the context of the school. It is not prescriptive and our hope is that educators will adapt the ideas and examples to their Early Childhood settings. We have used Drs. Diaspora in a variety of settings including all-Black, integrated, and majority-White settings. In all cases, children are left with positive and deep understandings that African-descendant people are not acultural. This is an important goal of Pro-Black pedagogy.

Key Components of Drs. Diaspora Curriculum

Two components are at the center of the Drs. Diaspora curriculum: (1) focusing on cultural continuity and (2) using African diaspora literacies to teach African diaspora literacy.

Focusing on cultural continuity. Drs. Diaspora aims to teach children how African values have existed across time—from ancient

Africa to contemporary times. Hence, in the title, we borrow from Egyptologist Anthony Browder and other Africanists' metaphor of rivers: *From the Nile to the Niger to Rivers in the U.S.* That is, Africa is the cradle of civilization, and when Africans migrated from Nile Valley civilization to West Africa to the United States, they carried their cultural legacies and values with them. Though they are dynamic and morph over time and space, these cultural legacies and values can be seen as, and are, important to the welfare of Black children and people.

We use Adinkra symbols from the Akan people as a proxy for African values (Boutte, 2022; Jackson et al., 2021). These symbols represent deep structural African values such as perseverance, courage, beauty, community, unity. There are hundreds of symbols. We recognize the variation among African cultures but choose to use these powerful symbolic images as tools for conveying African values that exist among African diasporic people. Gloria has taught teachers and students to use Adinkra symbols to teach African values. As seen in Chapters 3–9, our academic legacies (Jarvais J. Jackson, Saudah N. Collins, and Janice R. Baines) have found that these symbols can readily be used to convey African values to young children in their respective classrooms. Additionally, children remember the symbols and accompanying values—and apply them to their own lives.

Using African diaspora literacies to teach African diaspora literacy. Drawing from one of the *Ten Vital Principles for Black Education and Socialization* (King, 2005), we use Africancentric ways of knowing and integrate the arts and humanities in Drs. Diaspora activities. Here we use the term *African diaspora* **literacies** (nod to Janice R. Baines for this term) to connote African diasporic epistemologies or ways of knowing, being, and communicating. Hence, the pedagogical instructional style incorporates storytelling, role-playing, music, drumming, and interactive activities. For instance, using call-and-response, we begin class by saying, "Agoo!" The Akan (from Ghana) term *agoo* is used to ask for permission from the gathering to speak. The response to give consent to speak is *amee*. We go through several practice routines using this call-and-response strategy that will be used consistently throughout our residence as Drs. Diaspora historians.

Drs. Diaspora: Agoo!
Children: Amee!

Drs. Diaspora: Agoo! *(whispering)*
Children: Amee! *(whispering)*
Drs. Diaspora: Agoo! *(loudly)*
Children: Amee! *(loudly)*

Activities can be adapted by grade level, but general concepts taught will be the same. Teachers will find that most curriculum standards lend themselves to teaching Drs. Diaspora content. Informal, oral group assessments can be done before and after each lesson to see what students already know and what they have learned. Three websites with historical resources are listed below.

- Zinn Education Project (https://zinnedproject.org/)
- Rethinking Schools (https://www.rethinkingschools.org/index.shtml)
- Learning for Justice (https://www.learningforjustice.org/)

Background

Every summer since the oldest granddaughters (twins) were 4, Gloria has taught our grandchildren African and African history. We developed parts of the Drs. Diaspora curriculum in this way. We now have six grandchildren and counting: 17-year-old twins, a 12-year-old, a 9-year old, a 6-year-old, and a 5-month-old. Simultaneously, we conceptualized and taught Africancentric Saturday school for elementary students using the Drs. Diaspora curriculum. A planning grant from the South Carolina Humanities Council was also used to develop the curriculum for the Saturday Academy.

During a parent–teacher conference at our grandchildren's schools, we happened to mention that we teach the grandchildren African and African American history. The principal (Dr. Eunice Williams—a White female at the predominantly White school) mused, "They have artists in residence in schools. We should invite you all to be *historians in residence* since we all need this information." Thus, Drs. Diaspora curriculum materialized into a reality.

We piloted the program in April and May 2017 with all 4th- and 5th-graders ($n=85$) in a majority-White elementary school. There were four separate classes. Each class had a 50-minute slot that had previously been used for a dance class that had ended. Since then, we have used the 4-week version of the historians in residence

Drs. Diaspora curriculum in several elementary schools, two middle schools, and one high school.

Description of the Program

We use the theme of *sankofa*, an Akan term from Ghana, West Africa, which means to "go back and take" (*sanko-* go back, *fa-* take) or "It is not wrong to go back for that which you have forgotten" (http://en.wikipedia.org/wiki/Sankofa). In essence, we not only help students "look back" and learn the history of people in the African diaspora and the forebears of all humans, but we also helped them look forward by studying contemporary and future issues facing African-descent people. Because much of African and African American history has been left out of school curricula and textbooks, we emphasize that teaching children and ourselves the rich legacies of African thought can be a restorative and healing process—not only for people of African descent, but for humanity at large. It provides everyone with a more complete version of history. Sankofa's content and activities covers three major areas of focus.

1. Life for African Americans before enslavement
2. Life during initial contact with Europeans and European Americans and afterward
3. Contemporary life of Africans and African Americans (Boutte, 2016)

These are further broken down into six historical periods in the United States. These are presented sequentially and recursively. Throughout, Black historical consciousness themes mentioned in Chapter 1 are centered.

1. Ancient Africa and the African continent
2. Enslavement—Particular attention is paid to slave narratives, agency, and resistance of African people who were enslaved.
3. Reconstruction
4. Jim Crow—including the Harlem Renaissance in the 1920s
5. Civil Rights Era—Emphasis on Black nationalism, freedom schools, freedom songs, and student protests
6. Contemporary life in the United States and African diaspora worldwide

Sample Schedule (50 minutes—1½ hours)

5–15 minutes	Welcome basket (Roll Call; Sankofa Affirmation; Concept for the Day)
15–30 minutes	Griot storytelling/literature (African folklore; African American/African history; Ma'at, etc.)
25–35 minutes	Work on project of the day—e.g., dramatic presentation, writing assignment, Internet research, artwork
5–10 minutes	Sharing and wrap-up

Sample Themes

The curriculum is not meant to be prescriptive, but key to the lessons will be Africanisms that have been handed down through generations. Using 11 cultural dimensions of African and African American culture that have been cited in the literature, these legacies are integrated throughout using Adinkra symbols as proxies (Table 3.2).

Table 3.2. Dimensions of African American Culture

African American Cultural Dimension	Sample Themes, Activities, Books
1. *Spirituality*—an approach to life as being essentially vitalistic rather than mechanistic, with the conviction that nonmaterial forces influence people's everyday lives	• *What is your life purpose?* collage • *Connections between the past and the present* • *Ma'at philosophy* • Book: *Sense past king: A Story from Cameroon* (Tchana & Hyman, Holiday House, 2002)
2. *Harmony*—the notion that one's fare is interrelated with other elements in the scheme of things, so that humankind and nature are harmonically conjoined	• *Outside adventures and experiments* • Book: *African folk tales* (Vernon-Jackson, Dover Publications, 2012) • Book: *What a wonderful world* (Weiss, Thiele, & Bryan; Atheneum Books, 1995)
3. *Movement*—an emphasis on the interweaving of movement, rhythm, percussiveness, music, and dance, all of which are taken as central to psychological health	• *African dance* • *Role playing* • *Handplays* • Book: *Max found two sticks* (Pinkney, Aladdin, 1997)

(*continued*)

Table 3.2. *(continued)*

African American Cultural Dimension	Sample Themes, Activities, Books
4. *Verve*—a propensity for relatively high levels of stimulation and for action that is energetic and lively	• *Creative writing* • *Hip-hop pedagogy (flocabulary)*
5. *Affect*—an emphasis on emotions and feelings, together with a specific sensitivity to emotional cues and a tendency to be emotionally expressive	• *Dramatic play* • *Role-playing* • *Videotaping* • *Spoken word* • *Hip-hop pedagogy* • *Music (e.g., freedom songs and their meanings)* • *Art*
6. *Communalism/collectivity*—a commitment to social connectedness, which includes an awareness that social bonds and responsibilities transcend individual privilege	• *Group learning activities* • *Peer tutoring and scaffolding* • *Integrate information about Black communities and sages* • *Living history (bring in elders, sages, from community)* • *Ubuntu (I am because we are)* • *Book: Our children can soar* (Cook & Dillon, Bloomsbury, 2012)
7. *Expressive individualism*—the cultivation of a distinctive personality and proclivity for spontaneous, genuine personal expression	• *Assignments and projects will allow for multiple means of expression (e.g., videos, songs, collages, written papers, spoken word).*
8. *Oral tradition*—strengths in oral/aural modes of communication, in which both speaking and listening are treated as performances, and cultivation of oral virtuosity. The ability to use alliterative, metaphorically colorful, graphic forms of spoken language	• *Integrate oral traditions such as songs into routine activities such as attendance.* • *Use a variety of genres.* • *Debate and speaking skills* • *Talking drums* • *Featured and invited orators from Black communities* • *Well known orators (e.g., Malcolm X, Sojourner Truth, Martin Luther King, Septima Clark, Modjeska Simkins, Oprah Winfrey, Jay-Z, community members)* • *Books: The classic tales of Br'er Rabbit* (Harris, Running Press Kids, 2008)

(continued)

Table 3.2. (*continued*)

African American Cultural Dimension	Sample Themes, Activities, Books
9. *Social time perspective*—an orientation in which time is treated as passing through a social space rather than a material one, and in which time can be recurring, personal, and phenomenological. Time is acknowledged as a social construct.	• *Teach how indigenous people read signs from nature (e.g., moss, stars, blooms)* • *Valuing people and relationships (e.g., talking with others is not wasting time)* • *Book: So much!* (Cooke & Oxenbury, Candlewick, 2008) • *Book: Follow the drinking gourd* (Winter, Dragonfly Books, 1992)
10. *Perseverance*—ability to maintain a sense of agency and strength in the face of adversities	• *Examples of ancestors, family members, community members who persisted despite hardships* • *History of Mother Emanuel Church* • *Resistance, rebellions, and agency in Black communities* • *Narratives of enslaved Africans* • *Book: Moses: How Harriet Tubman led her people to freedom* (Weatherford & Nelson; Little, Brown; 2006) • *Book: Freedom on the menu* (Weatherford & Lagarrigue, Puffin Books, 2007) • *Book: The story of Ruby Bridges* (Coles & Ford, Scholastic, 2010)
11. *Improvisation*—substitution of alternatives that are more sensitive to Black culture	• *Allow for improvisation during lessons and on assignments.* • *Teach about historical improvisations (e.g., Denmark Vesey).* • *Common quilt patterns* • *Book: Light in the darkness* (Cline-Ransome & Ransome; Little, Brown, 2013) • *Book: New shoes* (Meyer & Velasquez, Holiday House, 2016) • *Book: I see rhythm* (Igus, Children's Book Press, 2005)

Source: Boutte, G. S. (2022). *Educating African American students: And how are the children?* Routledge. Adapted with permission.

Because of the elasticity of the two components (cultural continuity and African diaspora literacies), we are able to adapt key ideas for preschool through high school. Here we share a few examples of activities used with kindergartners, particularly since many ECE educators may wonder if 4- and 5-year-old children will engage with the content (Boutte & Strickland, 2008). We assure you—they do. We share a few sample resources that we use across the six historical periods. It is important to remember that actual lessons are more robust than what we describe since we only mention select activities for the purpose of demonstration.

For all ages, we transform the classroom by draping African fabric on a few tables, displaying books, putting up a timeline, posting maps of Africa (and the world with Africa drawn proportionally correct), and placing two djembe drums and a few other African instruments (e.g., balafon, shekere). We are usually adorned with African clothing and jewelry that capture children's attention immediately without even speaking.

We begin with Adinkra symbols and allow children to choose one (or more that appeal to them) and draw them with markers to make name placards (Figure 3.1).

We use these name placards for every session, and children keep them at the end of our time as historians in residence. We spend time discussing the meanings of the symbols and relating them to other topics throughout the 4-week period. Drumming and musical instruments are also integrated throughout, and **EVERY** session includes dancing or movement. Many of the books that we use are

Figure 3.1. Finished Name Placards

also available on YouTube via *Sankofa Read Alouds.* To learn about the continent, we use a YouTube video, *In My Africa,* which tells about the (then) 54 countries in Africa. The tune is catchy and we play it at the beginning of each session. At the end of each session, children have time to reflect and write or draw one thing they learn in blank books (that are filled at the end of all the sessions). This they keep and can share with families. Below we share just a *glimpse* of Drs. Diaspora activities for kindergartners with the hope that EC teachers are inspired to put their own spin and imprints on these ideas.

ANCIENT AFRICA AND THE AFRICAN CONTINENT

For young children, we've noted two of our favorite books below that have been particularly impactful because they present an overview of content to follow. Children identify with the young girls in the book (rest assured, we also use books with boy characters, and teachers should be intentional about balancing genders).

1. Medearis, A. S. (1994). *Our people.* Gingham Dog Press. This book features a young African American girl and her father as he walks her through some of the accomplishments of Black people (our people) from ancient Africa to modern times. After each description, the child imagines herself in the places. For example, when her dad describes the pyramids in ancient Egypt (Kemet), she and he are shown building pyramids with her blocks.
2. Mitchell, R. (1997). *Talking cloth.* Orchard Books. This book also features a young girl talking with her aunt and dad as her aunt describes her travels to Africa and explains how African cloths *talk* (carry messages). We use this to introduce children to the three fabrics introduced in the book: Adinkra, mudcloth, and kente. Children use Adinkra stamps to make patterns, create kente patterns using a variety of media, view short videos about how the fabrics were made, and on and on. Children create their own talking cloth. We put the book in conversation with other books like the following ones which

explains significance of kente colors, legends about its origin, and so forth.

- McDermott, G. (1987). *Anansi the spider: A tale from the Ashanti.* Henry Holt & Company
- Chocolate, D. (1996). *Kente colors.* Walker and Company.
- Musgrove, M. (2001). *The spider weaver: A legend of Kente cloth.* Scholastic.

Another favorite activity to teach about Africa is Drs. Diaspora Kente Mystery Bag (Figure 3.2). We include representations of some of Africa's nature resources. Children reach in the bag and pull out an item and try to guess what it represents. When they have pulled them all, we post them on a board with labels of each that serves as a reminder of Africa's nature resources. Since we also use PowerPoint slides, a sample slide can be seen in Figure 3.3 that guides children's discussion of the uses of the natural resources in our lives in the United States.

Figure 3.2. Drs. Diaspora Kente Mystery Bag

Figure 3.3. African Natural Resources Slide

Resources		Uses
Gold		
Rubber		
Diamonds	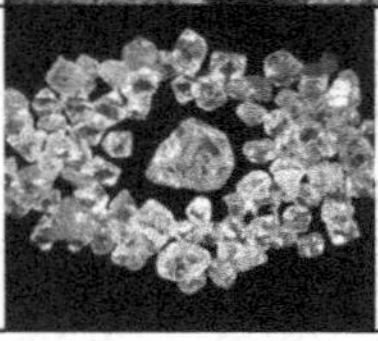	
Copper	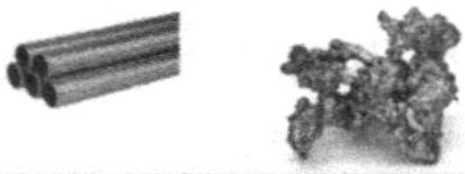	
Salt		
Oil		

ENSLAVEMENT

Our main goal is for children to know that Black people had and have agency. We show ways that African values show up during enslavement to make the point of cultural continuity. As we engage children in storytelling about the ancient kingdoms of Mali and mention kings, queens, and everyday people and families, we are adorned like African royalty with beads, rings, and jewelry, and a crown for Gloria and an African hat for George. Both of us have kente cloth draped over our shoulder. George also has a staff. As we tell the story of Africans being kidnapped and brought to the United States and other places, we simultaneously take off the adornments.

Two books that we use are listed.

1. Hannah-Jones, N., & Watson, R. (2021). *The 1619 project: Born on the water*. Penguin.
2. Cline-Ransome, L. (2013). *Light in the darkness. A story about how slaves learned in secret*. Jump At the Sun Publishers. We love that this book problematizes the idea that Black people were ignorant and could not read. It shows the great lengths that they went through to learn to read, despite dire consequences.

We introduce a few abolitionists—Black and White, men and women, national and local. We show how Africans read signs in nature (such as the stars and migration of birds) and symbols to escape. We discuss revolts by people who were enslaved. One activity uses photos from Frederick Douglass's anti-slavery campaign that depicts counternarrative portraits of Black people in a variety of positive roles. Black people are shown as productive citizens and "normal" people. In small groups, children think about a slogan for one photo (e.g., what do you think the person is trying to express?) and try to find an Adinkra value/symbol to relate to the photo. The collection is available from the website *Mirror of Race* (2023). We laminated the photos for reuse.

RECONSTRUCTION

Highlights of some of the lessons on reconstruction include gallery walks of photos of Black free towns during and soon after enslavement. It is fascinating for children to see this positive imagery and agency among Black people during this time period. This narrative is rarely included in schools. In groups, children study a photo of their choice and write/draw an Adinkra value that the photo reminds them of. We also show Black legislators, businesspeople, and a host of successful African Americans during this time, amplifying the tremendous productivity that was interrupted by the Jim Crow era.

Since we live in South Carolina and most children's families know the University of South Carolina (USC) Gamecocks football team, we use this opportunity to show photos of groups of Black students enrolled at USC during reconstruction. We explain that, unlike today, USC was majority Black and was closed down for 3 years because of that. USC did not admit Black students again until 1963. We show well-known photos of the first three Black students to be admitted in the 20th century (Henrie D. Monteith, Robert Anderson, and James Solomon) and also photos of Gloria (who teaches at USC) receiving awards from two USC presidents. We show pictures of Dr. Richard T. Greener, the university's first African American professor who taught at USC during reconstruction. We narrate that these 12 years of reconstruction demonstrated the agency and persistence of Black people.

We engage children in rich dialogue by asking questions like the following.

- After African Americans who were enslaved were freed, what laws do you think needed to be passed to ensure that they would be treated fairly?
- What resources (unpack as needed) would African Americans need to help them start their new lives?
- What help would be needed for White southerners?

We discuss the idea of reparations and *40 acres and a mule*. We explain that much of the land in beach towns like Hilton Head was given to Black people who were freed after the Civil War. We also learn and watch videos of the Black national anthem, "Lift Every Voice and Sing," which was written during this period. These are a few samples of activities for this era. *Flocabulary* has an excellent video on the Thirteenth, Fourteenth, and Fifteenth Amendments that we use with 4th-graders and higher. EC educators should research local successes during this period in their respective states to make examples more concrete. We recommend these four children's books.

1. Cline-Ransome, L. (2015). *Freedom's school*. Little, Brown Books for Young Readers.
2. Lyons, K. S. (2012). *Ellen's broom*. G. P. Putnam's Sons Books for Young Readers.

3. Miller, E. A. (2008). *Gullah statesman: Robert Smalls from slavery to congress, 1839–1915*. University of South Carolina Press.
4. Turner, A. (2015). *My name is truth: The life of Sojourner Truth*. Harper Collins.

JIM CROW (ERA)

We usually begin this segment by reading *New Shoes* (Myers, 2015). Children can relate to wanting and buying new shoes that the young girl in the story experiences. We discuss the intergenerational African values that the girls (main character and friend) in the story used. Children draw pictures of what they would do if they were discriminated against. A few books are offered for this era.

1. Deans, K. (2015). *Swing sisters*. The story of the international sweethearts of rhythm. Holiday House. This book is a bit long so may read pictures to younger children.
2. Johnson, D. (1998). *All around the town. The photographs of Richard Samuel Roberts*. Henry Holt & Company.
3. Lawrence, J. (1993). *The great migration: An American story*. Harper Collins.
4. Myers, S. L. (2015). *New shoes*. Holiday House.
5. Myers, W. D. (1997). *Harlem. A poem by Walter D. Myers*. Scholastic. Each page of this lively, beautiful book is a lesson in itself. Teachers can spend time on one or two pages per day rather than read the entire book, which may need unpacking for young children.
6. Weatherford, C. B. (2021). *Unspeakable: The Tulsa race massacre*. Carol Rhoda Books.

BLACK NATIONALIST/ CIVIL RIGHTS ERA

We emphasize Freedom Schools and share some of the songs used in current Children's Defense Fund Children's School such as "Something Inside So Strong" by Labri Siffre. We find videos on YouTube of children performing the song. We share other freedom songs such as "We Shall Overcome," coupled with video essays, featuring young children. We feature Black people's organizations and discuss African values such as unity and interdependence and remind children of examples across time and space (e.g., ancient Africa to present).

We use a photo of a Black girl and White girl in a classroom at the beginning of integration and deliberate on what they think each girl was thinking. A few of our favorite books are listed below.

1. Brann, S. K. (2017). *The ABCs of the Black Panther party*. Decolonizing Education Publishing.
2. Bridges, R. (2016). *Ruby Bridges goes to school: My true story*. Scholastic.
3. Clark-Robinson, M. (2018). *Let the children march*. HMH Books for Young Readers.
4. Coleman, E. (1996). *White socks only*. Albert Whitman.
5. Coles, R. (1995). *The story of Ruby Bridges*. Scholastic.
6. Johnson, A. (2007). *A sweet smell of roses*. Simon & Schuster Books for Young Readers.

CONTEMPORARY LIFE IN THE AFRICAN DIASPORA

Because young children's sense of time is still developing, we want to ensure that they understand that Black people and Black culture are not something only in the past. As Black people, we are here now in contemporary times and we are cultural beings. We emphasize cultural continuities and point out similarities across time and contexts—not only in the United States but worldwide. We want them to know that Black culture is robust and dynamic.

We show pictures of various places in the diaspora from our travels (e.g., continent of Africa, Caribbean, South America). We have activities where we look at monies from these places and have children design their own currencies, emphasizing that the monies feature people who represent their cultures. We use a series of Nigerian books by author Ifeoma Onyefulu (www.ifeomaonyefuluco.uk/), which depict young children in school, playing games, getting haircuts, and other daily activities, and involved in families and communities. We interrupt stereotypes about Africa only being home to animals and people living only in huts by showing images of cities and small town with a variety of house types. We discuss Kwanzaa as a contemporary holiday that encompasses African history and present-day life in the United States and in Africa, and do several related activities and listen to songs. Another book that children like is:

- Robinson, A. (2020). *The modern day Black alphabet.* Arial Robinson.

CULMINATING ACTIVITIES

In small groups, children focus on one of the six major time periods. Each group is given premade blank books to write in. For their assigned time period, students will draw pictures and describe one thing that they remember or know about the time period or the African or African American people. They also write/draw one challenge that the people faced during this time period. They draw one Adinkra symbol that represents the African value that helped the Africans or African Americans deal with the challenge and write what the Adinkra symbol means. Groups will share what they wrote and drew with the rest of the class. We conclude the lesson by talking about sankofa (the importance of knowing the past in order to understand the future).

CHAPTER 4

I'll Take You There
Envisioning and Sustaining African Diasporic Educational Spaces

Jarvais J. Jackson

*I know a place
Ain't nobody cryin'
Ain't nobody worried
Ain't no smilin' faces*

—The Staple Singers, 1972

In the 1970s hit "I'll Take You There," the Staple Singers (1972) envisioned an oasis where there is a break from the cares of the world. As they sang about this place, many of us smiled and envisioned what it would be like to visit this idyllic place. Indeed, during my education experiences in K–12 schools and in my undergraduate program, I yearned for refuge in such a place where no one was worrying or crying. In this chapter, I revise and extrapolate the theme and lyrics of "I'll Take You There" to guide my reflections on educational spaces that honor Black children's culture.

*I know a place
Black students are learnin'
Black students are loved
Black students are proud to be BLACK*

In this chapter, I share a classroom where the vision of cultural and academic excellence among Black students is a reality. This is a place where Black students learn to be racially literate about themselves and other African-descendant people. I invite readers to join me on a virtual field trip to a Pro-Black elementary African studies classroom. My hope is that readers will return from this excursion in this chapter renewed, refreshed, and inspired to implement Pro-Black pedagogies in Early Childhood settings.

Before venturing into the field trip, I introduce myself (your tour guide) by describing my vision for Pro-Black spaces and my positionality. I uplift African diaspora literacy as a Pro-Black pedagogy. Next, I share the context of the K–5 African studies classroom that embodies the joyful Black place I envision. I conclude with a call to action for readers to work toward the facilitation of transformative, affirming Pro-Black teaching for Black children.

DREAMING OF A PLACE: RESEARCHER POSITIONALITY

Like most teacher education programs in the United States, mine contained limited representation of Black people's perspectives and experiences. It felt like I needed to assimilate to achieve success, even though my Black soul was not at ease. Supposedly, we were learning how to teach *all* students; yet the only thing we learned about teaching Black students was how they were not reaching benchmarks that other students met. Rather than addressing the educational debt owed to Black students or the opportunity gap (Ladson-Billings, 2006; Milner, 2012), teacher education programs and K–12 schools continue to hide under the guise of an "achievement gap" that inherently problematizes Black children (Ford et al., 2008; Howard, 2019; Ladson-Billings, 2006; Milner, 2012; Singham, 2003). Few, if any, strategies for liberating and honoring Black students' culture are shared. Reflecting on my discomfort during my teacher education program coursework and in K–12 school, I understand how uncomfortable Black children must be in typical classrooms.

During my studies at my predominantly White university, I frequently questioned what could and should be done to address the academic and cultural needs of Black students. The lack of viable solutions left me dreaming of a redemptive place where Black students were liberated through the honoring of their cultures rather than being traumatized by irrelevant curriculum, assaultive disciplinary practices, and placement policies that negatively profile them (Baines et al., 2018; Boutte, 2016; King, 1992, 2005; Jackson et al., 2021; Woodson, 1933).

Understanding that Black culture and histories were missing from what I was being taught, I yearned for a place where Black children could bring their whole selves. My dream was a dream of liberation from oppressive educational systems that continue to impede Black children's ability to reach academic and cultural excellence. While I did not have the words to describe my vision as an undergraduate student, I later understood I was dreaming of a place where Pro-Black pedagogies were foundational to teaching. While Pro-Black pedagogy is not prescriptive and can be achieved in different ways, I have found that using African diaspora literacy can be a powerful teaching pedagogy.

AFRICAN DIASPORA LITERACY

As discussed in Chapter 1, African diaspora literacy (ADL) is the reclamation of the stories of African diasporic people (Johnson et al., 2018a; King, 1992). It is a source of humanity, liberation, and healing (Boutte et al., 2017; King, 1992). Drawing from Boutte et al.'s (2017) conception of ADL as becoming literate about Black people wherever they are in the world, we understand that Africa is the place that connects Black people throughout the globe.

African diaspora literacy serves as opposition to the literacies that exclude and distort Black knowledges and histories by centering African knowledges (Boutte et al., 2017; Jackson et al., 2021). ADL embraces the beauty and brilliance of Blackness without comparison to any other cultural group. Rather than constructing their lives based on Eurocentric standards and epistemologies, Black students, like any other race, should learn about themselves first (Woodson, 1933). Yet typical school curricula are filled with Eurocentric ideas and beliefs (Baines et al., 2018; Boutte, 2016; Boutte et al., 2017). African diaspora literacy embraces the Black cultural dimensions, Black home languages, and other Black cultural expressions such as dress, music, and so much more. While ADL focuses on Black knowledges, it also benefits students from other ethnic groups since it is an antidote to inaccurate and distorted histories about African-descendant people.

In Pro-Black contexts where ADL thrives, children engage in curricular and pedagogical practices that embrace their identities as Black people. Educational excellence is achieved, and students can live in their divine purposes, uninterrupted by ongoing cultural assaults. I provide a description of an African diasporic literacy classroom that illuminates my vision of an ECE classroom where Black children's humanity is welcomed and supported.

Again, African diaspora literacy instruction is nonprescriptive. While similarities among teachers using ADL pedagogy are readily apparent, the needs of the students are different; therefore, teachers approach instruction in different ways. Likewise, teachers bring their unique selves and vibes to their teaching.

PRO-BLACKNESS IN ECE SETTINGS

Black-affirming spaces are not singular places. There are many Pro-Black classrooms that manifest this metaphoric place[1] that I envisioned. Here I introduce readers to one such space.

Ms. Saudah N. Collins is an African American teacher of African studies for K–5th-graders. I focus on her instruction with K–3 children for this chapter but emphasize that Pro-Black settings are important for *all* grade levels. Ms. Collins is affiliated with the Center for the Education and Equity of African American Students (CEEAAS) and was selected because of her consistent demonstration of achieving cultural and academic excellence for African American students (Boutte, 2022). I observed Ms. Collins during the fall 2021 semester, visiting her class weekly for 3-hour sessions. I also conducted interviews to gain more information about her teaching and to clarify my observations.

Context

Ms. Collins teaches at a majority-Black elementary school in the southeastern United States, comprised of approximately 77% African American students, 13% Hispanic, 8% two or more races, 1% Asian, and 1% White. Males and females represent about 50 percent each. Approximately 82% of students receive benefits such as Temporary Assistance for Needy Families (TANF), Medicaid, and Supplemental Nutrition Assistance Program (SNAP). Some students are identified as foster children, homeless, or migrants.

The school is in a district with a superintendent who prioritized culturally relevant and sustaining instruction. The district hosts professional development on culturally relevant pedagogy and supports teachers' and administrators' participation in national professional development on anti-racist teaching and culturally relevant and sustaining teaching. Likewise, the school's principal upholds the same expectation of meeting students' needs through comprehensive and culturally relevant instruction that honors students' lives and pushes them toward academic and cultural excellence. The principal, Dr. Sabina Mosso-Taylor, initiated the implementation of the school's African studies program, the first of its kind in the district and state at the elementary school level. She handpicked Ms. Collins to teach the course because of her commitment to African diaspora literacy pedagogy. After observing Ms. Collins's teaching using ADL in her 1st- and 2nd-grade classrooms over a 2-year period, Dr. Mosso-Taylor wanted all the students in the school to benefit from this instruction.

Ms. Saudah N. Collins is a veteran teacher of over 30 years. She has worked as a teacher in multiple roles in general education and special education classrooms, as a university liaison on a multimillion-dollar grant serving schools statewide, as a teacher interventionist, as a National Board liaison, and as a preservice teacher educator—among a litany of other things. She has been recognized nationally as a recipient of the Presidential Award for Mathematics and Science Teaching, a Gilder Lehrman Institute of American History State Social Studies Teacher of the Year and National finalist, and a National Elementary Social Studies teacher.

Working as a graduate assistant with the Center for the Education and Equity of African American Students (CEEAAS), I had the privilege of observing teachers as part of ongoing research projects. While I met Ms. Collins during my time teaching at the same school, I never got to experience her teaching. In my notes during my first visit, I wrote, "I have never seen someone teach like this" (fieldnotes, August 29, 2018). I was seeing my vision of an empowering Black space. At the time she was teaching 1st grade. Ms. Collins, cool, calm, and collected in nature, commanded the respect of her students with such grace. She treated her students with love, and they returned that to her and their peers. I was in awe that Ms. Collins was able to engage 1st-graders in African diasporic literacy. From day one, she included families, and immersed both the students and their families in ADL content and activities as they built foundational skills. During the school's orientation, she captured a photo of each family and placed it on a tree that extended across a wall in the classroom. As families join throughout the year, she asks for a photo to include. Students are reminded that their family is a part of the classroom community. Below I describe Ms. Collins's classroom using a theme that represents the classroom overall based on analyses of the data collected during the semester.

A Trip to Africa—A Journey of Blackness—Ms. Collins's Classroom. Akwaaba! This is the greeting one receives when visiting Ms. Collins's classroom. This Twi greeting from the Akan culture of West Africa means *welcome*. Ms. Collins teaches a required course on African studies for all K–5 students at her school. In her unique role, she can define her curriculum and content. With over 30 years of experience in the classroom, she is knowledgeable of the content covered in general education classrooms to connect with African diasporic content.

Ms. Collins emphasizes cultural competence within her class. In many cases, it might be assumed that this involves becoming competent about cultures beyond the students' world. However, in this case, the goal is for all students, particularly Black students, to understand Black culture and histories better. She explained, "all pedagogy is relevant to someone's culture. We just got to make sure it's relevant to those students who are often underserved and misrepresented." For students from other cultural groups, her class provides *windows* into Black culture and *sliding glass doors* (Bishop, 1990), which extend their imaginations and immerse them in Black culture.

Readers traveling with me to Ms. Collins's Pro-Black space should open the *sliding glass doors* in their minds and imagine being in the classroom. Three areas of focus that are instructive to prospective Pro-Black educators are highlighted: (1) classroom decor; (2) integration of Black cultural dimensions; and (3) Pro-Black pedagogy and content. Readers will note the overlapping and recursive nature of these three aspects.

Pro-Black decor in the classroom. Heeding Woodson's (1933) assertion that the education of any group of people should begin with themselves, Ms. Collins's classroom has multiple positive images of Black people since African American students make up three-quarters of the school. One glance at her classroom provides a taste of six historical periods described in the Drs. Diaspora curriculum in

Figure 4.1. African Artifacts Displayed in Ms. Collins' Class

Chapter 3: (1) Ancient Africa, (2) Enslavement, (3) Reconstruction, (4) Jim Crow/Segregation, (5) Civil Rights/Black Nationalism, and (6) Contemporary Life Among Africans in the Diaspora.

African fabrics line the tables and student spaces. One bookshelf is topped with enough African musical instruments to start a small band, and another features Adinkra symbols (from the Akan people of West Africa), stamps, and coasters (shown in Figure 4.1).

Above the bulletin boards, a golden silhouette of the continent of Africa is displayed. An "A is for Africa" poster starts the trail seen throughout the classroom. These posters include various African people, dishes, games, languages, and traditions. They serve as the anchor of the word wall[2] often required by districts that continues to grow throughout the year. These are not mere artifacts or classroom decor, but they bring the lessons to life for students. These are also active tools in the classroom community to allow students to experience learning. Symbolically, these decor accents send a message that Black culture is important.

In one corner, bold colors display the emblems and mascots of Historically Black Colleges and Universities (HBCUs) (shown in Figure 4.2). This corner includes photos of familiar faces of various teachers in the school posed receiving their degrees from HBCUs. There are also photos of teachers meeting Black authors such as Robert Constant, the author of *Hey Tuskegee* (Constant & Zeger, 2018). Other images show members of Black Greek Letter Organizations (BGLO) wearing their crests. Books by Black authors and illustrators are displayed around the classroom and used often. These books canvass Boutte's (2016; 2022) six historical periods from Ancient to Contemporary Africa and African Americans (shown in Figure 4.2).

Figure 4.2. Pro-Black Decor in the Classroom

Integration of Black cultural dimensions. Ensuring that students receive a more accurate view of Africa, Ms. Collins tells them, "We are starting with the people, not the animals."[3] One student shared his perspective of Africa through experience with movies and other media. He emphasized that his only account of Africa was as one big safari. This distorted view, along with others, catalyzes Ms. Collins's instructional efforts to correct miseducation about Africa and African diasporic people. Dillard (2012) referred to this as *re-membering*—the act of reclaiming African indigenous knowledges (King & Swartz, 2014).

Ms. Collins engages with the students in a comforting manner. She refers to the 700+ students as her children (communalism) and relies on her "motherly" intuition, evident through her soft but firm nature with the students, often kneeling to get on the same level as them yet being insistent and conveying expectations. She greets each student by name and addresses them as future lawyers, doctors, and other professionals as she explains how they might use the information they are learning in her class and their other classes (spirituality). She connects with students using African American Language (AAL) throughout instruction (orality). For example, when establishing the classroom expectations, Ms. Collins assures students that she "be lovin' black children"[4] (Boutte et al., 2021b). Jordan (1988) explained that many Black children rely on AAL to explore the world and make meaning. As a result, Black children thrive in environments where they are not forced to hide their language identity (Baines et al., 2018). During some lessons, she asks for an amen from the "amen corner," an African American church reference (spirituality).

Ms. Collins's use of AAL, coupled with the frequent use of music and space for students to dance and express themselves (movement, verve), creates an environment of comfort and joy. During the first couple of weeks of the school year, she opened the class with Mase's (2004) song "Welcome Back." As the song played, Ms. Collins told students they could groove to the music. Students' bodies moved as if they were listening to a favorite and familiar song. One student could barely get through the classroom door the following week before eagerly asking, "We gonna listen to the welcome back song?" During a following lesson, a West African music video was playing as background music; one student made a connection to a pop culture dance, the "stanky leg." Ms. Collins allowed the student to demonstrate the dance for the class. While listening to music, students are invited to drum along on their desk or lap. Often, I would see students with enormous smiles as they drummed to the beat of the music. As I watched them engage in the music and dance, I realized I was experiencing that place I dreamed of—a joyful, engaged Pro-Black classroom space. This was a place where students felt free to be themselves, which opened their minds to learning. No frustrations and worries were observed among the students, and, likewise, I was experiencing pure joy and learning African diasporic content at the same time.

The use of dancing and music is one example of how Ms. Collins blends in the legacies and dimensions of Black culture (Boutte, 2016; 2022; Boutte et al., 2017; Boykin, 1994). These common, intergenerational cultural strengths and legacies are shared among people in the African diaspora, including spirituality, harmony, movement, verve, affect, communalism, expressive individualism, and oral tradition. Ensuring these legacies and dimensions are a part of classroom instruction is an aspect of the healing nature of African diaspora literacy through the re-membering of history (Boutte et al., 2017; Dillard, 2012; King & Swartz, 2014). Ms. Collins routinely integrates Africanized legacies and dimensions into her instruction.

There are times when Ms. Collins revisits expectations. After being absent, she felt it necessary to have students engage in dialogue about misbehaviors exhibited with the substitute teacher. Rather than reprimanding students, she engaged them in conversation to understand the behaviors, giving them an opportunity to self-correct rather than being punished (spiritual). This honors the communal and redemptive nature of their class.

Pro-Black pedagogy and content. Instead of teaching the African studies content in isolation (disconnected from what students are learning in their regular classes), Ms. Collins weaves strategies from schoolwide programs in her instruction. Referring to the schoolwide engagement in the Advancement Via Individual Determination (AVID) program, she explains, "I just Africanize it." Here she uses the strategies available through programs such as AVID and matches them with African knowledges, principles, and content. Students are used to AVID strategies from their general education classes. They can apply those same methods to the content in African studies. For

Figure 4.3. Students Decorating Their Learning Portfolios

example, after a topic or unit in her class, Ms. Collins has the students complete a one-pager (summary). One-pagers are an AVID strategy to summarize students' learning on a singular page. They are used to synopsize each unit within African studies. Students are encouraged to put key themes and elements that piqued their interest on one-pagers. These themes can come from videos, activities, readings, and lectures to summarize their learning. For instance, one student drew a fan with African designs that Ms. Collins shared from her trip to Ghana, stating that it reminded her (student) of "church fans." One-pager requirements are based on grade level, so you will see more photos and single words for Early Childhood students. Figure 4.3 shows a student creating a one-pager showing their knowledge of the colors of the Pan-African flag and Kwanzaa; the student also included Adinkra symbols that correlated to their understanding of Kwanzaa and Pan-Africanism.

For young learners, particularly kindergarten and 1st-grade students, Ms. Collins focuses heavily on the developmental skills that they are working on in their general education classes. Africanizing it, she pairs these skills on African regions that are being covered within the course, often using music and dance to keep their young

Figure 4.4. Students Holding Up Their Pages in Alphabet Book

bodies and minds engaged (movement, verve). For example, kindergarten students collectively created an alphabet book that connects their learning of the alphabet and sounds with the African diaspora (communalism) (see Figure 4.4). Guiding her planning for K–1 learners, she states,

> I'm always thinking about as a 5- or 6-year-old learner, who is just starting out in a formalized school setting for some of them. And for them, both coming from households where primarily African American languages are spoken or Spanish or some French, how can I make our classroom feel like home? Always emphasizing the love, the joy, and our humaneness because that's another important part is that we're all human (S. Collins, personal communication, August 28, 2022).

Ms. Collins uses a lot more visuals with young learners (e.g., Google Earth when discussing continents and countries). She uses the opportunity to point out that Gladys Mae West, a Black woman mathematician, was instrumental in the development of satellite models used in GPS systems. When using photos and videos from Africa, Ms. Collins acknowledges the importance of allowing primary voices to stay dominant. She uses videos that have speakers talking in their native languages, with captions and narration to facilitate children's understanding. In all that she does, her goal is to connect the content to the lives of children. She also encourages children always to be ready to learn something new.

I'll Take You There   83

Because of the centrality of intergenerational African values for Black sustenance and healing, Ms. Collins (like other educators whose teaching coheres around Drs. Diaspora curriculum discussed in Chapter 3), Adinkra symbols are central to Pro-Black teaching in Ms. Collins's class. Adinkra symbols, globally recognized, are created by the Akan people of Ghana and Cote d'Ivoire (Jackson et al., 2021; Owusu, 2019).

Children in Ms. Collins's class use Adinkra symbols, connecting them to the various topics taught in the class. They first learned about Adinkra symbols and their origin and traditional uses at the beginning of the school year and have continued since. Ms. Collins introduced Adinkra symbols using the symbol *gye w'ani*, which means "enjoy yourself" or "joy." She encouraged students to think about what brings them joy in their lives. Adinkra symbols visually represent values and principles that connect to a myriad of relatable values such as spirituality and courage. Adinkra symbols are one of many sign systems on the continent of Africa that can be used in elementary classrooms.

As the year progressed, the students used Adinkra symbols in various ways. Each lesson begins with an Adinkra symbol and its corresponding value. As the classroom community was established during the first few weeks, Ms. Collins started the lesson with the symbol *nea onnim no sua a, ohu*—"He who does not know can know from learning." A slide from her lesson featuring the Adinkra symbol is displayed in Figure 4.5.

Figure 4.5. Adinkra Symbol, *Nea Onnim No Sua A, Ohu*

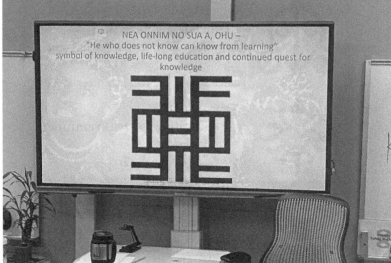

Children decorated their name tents and learning portfolios using Adinkra symbols representing personal values, classrooms' values, communities' values, and families' values. They also use Adinkra symbols when analyzing characteristics or traits of people, places, and processes discussed during various learning explorations in African studies. For example, when children analyze the lyrics to songs or the behaviors of individuals discussed or read about, they then use Adinkra symbols as a part of that analysis. Children use the symbols based on the meanings/values to describe the clear message. Some examples of Adinkra symbols are shared in Figure 4.6.

Figure 4.6. Adinkra Symbol Examples

Sankofa
go back and get it

Dweninmmen
strength (in mind, body, and soul)

Odo Nnyew Fie Kwan
love does not lose its way home

Funtumfunefu Denkyemfunefu
unity in diversity

Akoma Ntoaso
the joining of hearts

Figure 4.7. Students Decorating Their Learning Portfolios

Throughout the school year, children use a portfolio to organize their learning in Ms. Collins's class. Their notes may take the form of brief entries on index cards, drawings, maps, graphic organizers, and connections using Adinkra symbols. The portfolios also include the one-pagers they create throughout the year and are designed to be a resource for students in the class and as they continue to learn and educate others about the African diaspora. Examples of children decorating their learning portfolios with Adinkra symbols can be seen in Figure 4.7. Students can add additional symbols, words, or drawings throughout the year—a space for their expressive individualism.

This portfolio can metaphorically be seen as a passport of sorts as children journey from Africa to Columbia, SC, where they live. Ms. Collins's class exceeds my imagination, as it takes Black children and others to a place I didn't even know existed. Their African diasporic journeys provide them with the opportunity to feel, hear, and sense Blackness all day long. The content that Ms. Collins uncovers represents a knowledge base that I was only recently introduced to as an adult and one that I am still learning.

CREATING MORE PRO-BLACK SPACES—IMPLICATIONS

Ms. Collins's classroom is an example of my dream of teachers who create a place where Black students are *learning, loved,* and *proud to be BLACK.* While she is only one example of the many ways

ADL can be implemented in classrooms, there are lessons that can be learned from her. Ms. Collins exhibits the full African and Black experience from decor to her use of the legacies and dimensions of African culture. She meets the needs of children, but the classroom is also reflective of her personality and lived experiences. Observing children in her classroom, I saw engagement, joy, and their conversations and work are evidence of the development of literacy about Black people and histories.

Calling teacher educators and educators to action, I employ readers to examine ways to incorporate African diaspora literacy in classrooms beyond the examples shared. Examples shared from Ms. Collins's classroom exhibit how ADL is woven through interdisciplinary instruction and content. Ms. Collins is an expert who has spent countless hours studying and immersing herself in ADL scholarship, professional development, and communities of teachers doing the same work. This is an important starting point for educators wishing to create classroom havens where Black culture is deeply embraced as a routine aspect of teaching.

Engaging in this work requires independent study and reliance on literary works and histories beyond content taught in P-20 settings. It is shameful and debilitating that I was in my graduate studies before I engaged in learning about Black histories that extend beyond surface-level understanding. Reading texts such as *The Miseducation of the Negro* (Woodson, 1933) metamorphosed my thinking and understanding. Students who are fortunate to have teachers such as Ms. Collins will be above par in their knowledge of Black histories, culture, and ways of being. To date, most Black children do not experience such learning in their P-12 experiences. Teacher preparation programs should be mindful of this deficit when preparing teachers, filling this gap with coursework that honors Black histories and culture.

I echo the call from scholars such as Carter G. Woodson, Joyce King, and Gloria Swindler Boutte for a transformation of educational space so Black students can develop self-love opposing the hegemonic histories and perspectives traditionally taught in P-20 educational spaces. These classes are what I dreamed of. My metaphoric nightmares associated with trauma I experienced in K–20 educational settings have been soothed with dreams of Black-affirming spaces like the ones created by Ms. Collins. In my dream, I smile as I envision classrooms likes theirs spreading like wildfire all over the world. It is my hope that African diasporic educational spaces become the standard for classrooms, fully supporting the cultural needs of Black students.

I know a place
Black students are learnin'
Black students are loved
Black students are proud to be BLACK

CHAPTER 5

Africanizing the Early Childhood Curriculum
Exploring Pro-Blackness Through African Diaspora Literacy

Saudah N. Collins

"I like black because when it is nighttime, it is dark. All around my house is black. I like black because my skin is Black. I like black because black is fantastic."

—"Black," written by Isaiah, 1st grade, 2018–2019

Like Isaiah, I love the color black and the cultural experiences of Blackness! As a young Black girl, my family planted and nurtured the seeds of pro-Blackness deep within me. For example, my dad, a Black Muslim, and my older sister chose the Arabic name Saudah Niema, not wanting a European moniker. My family followed Indigenous African practices of using natural, plant-based remedies to promote good health. They taught me to patronize Black businesses in the community, and we learned stories about contributions of Black people. The importance of the Black family was stressed. As a teacher, I witnessed the transformation of my young students, who learned to love and appreciate themselves more deeply, their communities, and the roots and sustained cultures of Blackness.

I be lovin' Black children, using the habitual *be* of African American Language to express that I loved them in the past; I love them in the present; I will continue to love them in the future. I have always chosen to teach in spaces where students who identified as Black or African American were in the majority. During the first 10 years of my career, 55% of the students of my first school identified as Black or African American. During the second 10 years, over 90% of the students identified as Black or African American in my second school setting; and for the last six years, over 80% of the students identify as Black or African American. I know that Pro-Black practices are important for all students regardless of their racialized identities. They are particularly important for children who identify as Black and African American because society often explicitly or implicitly embraces and perpetuates anti-Blackness, which negatively impacts all students. So, learning spaces, regardless of the percentages of African American students, must embrace Pro-Blackness unapologetically.

Early in my career, I was not a teacher who centered pro-Blackness in my pedagogy. By my early twenties, I unknowingly moved away from the earliest teachings of my parents. When I started teaching in the mid-1990s, I was multicultural in my pedagogical practices. I focused more on ensuring multiple cultures were represented (in my lessons) than deeply examining the children's cultures and making curriculum connections. For example, I overemphasized the value of students sitting quietly, only raising their hand to answer or ask questions, and using standardized English. I was an effective Early Childhood teacher in many ways, but there was room for deep reflection and growth. As a graduate student, I later learned about culturally relevant pedagogy (Ladson-Billings, 1995) and African diaspora literacy (Boutte et al., 2017) in preparation for my first trip to the continent of Africa in 2017. I progressively made the shift toward deepening my knowledge, transforming my pedagogical practices to embrace Pro-Blackness and alleviate assimilationist, anti-Black practices.

MY APPROACH

My pedagogical decisions are rooted in culturally relevant pedagogy, which has three tenets: academic success, cultural competence, and critical consciousness (Ladson-Billings, 1995). Rudine Sims Bishop's scholarship emphasized the importance of educators providing mirrors (affirmations of children's cultures) and windows (perspectives beyond children's worldviews) (Harris, 2007). Each decision was not a neutral one. I was intentional about what I taught and how I taught it. When making decisions about the educational experiences of the young learners, I was deeply reflective about the *who*, the *what*, the *why*, and the *how*. Guided by the cultural competence tenet of culturally relevant pedagogy, I always seek to affirm Black children's cultural identities using Pro-Black strategies. I used African diaspora literacy (ADL) to accomplish this goal.

Boutte et al. (2017) explained ADL's origins and healing power. When it is centered in classrooms and the lives of Black people, it offers an antidote for the ways in which our humanities and spirits are harmed by anti-Black experiences (Johnson & Bryan, 2018). Johnson et al. (2019) assert that ADL helps to reestablish the kinship connection to the continent and provides healing of the soul. Pro-Blackness, healing, and love are foundational to African diasporic learning experiences and explorations. Children are able to develop an understanding of who they are and can root their existence in connections to Africa, their ancestral home. These culturally relevant and humanizing practices are needed because of the ways in which traditional instructional practices center Whiteness and propagate anti-Blackness.

There is power in understanding and loving Blackness. This requires centering Black experiences and ancestral roots of Blackness as foundational to children's educational experiences. Below I explain how I engage our students, regardless of their racialized identities so that they embrace Blackness as fantastic and powerful.

The learning experiences described throughout this chapter represent my 20 years of work with young children as a pre-kindergarten, kindergarten, 1st-, 2nd-, and 3rd-grade teacher as well as 2 years of work as an African studies teacher for grades K–5. My learning experiences centered the power of Black love, joy, connectedness, brilliance, creativity, and ancestral knowledge. My approach to teaching and learning is a part of my spiritual healing as a Black woman who teaches Black children and other racialized groups. Black children embody love, joy, connectedness, creativity, and brilliance and are a reflection of their ancestral roots. In early childhood spaces, it is our responsibility to nurture and build on all the spirit and beauty and greatness that is already there. Young children come to us full of energy, full of life, and full of curiosity, and Early Childhood settings can amplify what they already bring through Pro-Black practices or extinguish it with anti-Blackness. It is important that we make emotional and physical spaces for the beauty and brilliance of Black children. That starts before they walk in the door for their first meeting with us as teachers. As an Early Childhood educator, I think deeply about what will make the early childhood space a place where love, joy, meaningful learning, and connectedness can abound. I focus on these questions: (1) What will the students see as they enter the door? (2) What will they hear? (3) How will they feel? (4) What freedom will they be able to embrace in the ways they use their bodies and minds? (5) Will they feel celebrated? (6) Will they see themselves reflected? And (7) Will the emotional and physical spaces be places where they thrive as they embody their full selves?

AFRICANIZE IT! HARNESSING THE POWER OF BLACKNESS THROUGH THE DEVELOPMENT OF AFRICAN DIASPORA LITERACY

At the heart of Pro-Black humanizing practices is exploring what it means to be human. We are all human. African diaspora literacy grounds our humanness (humanity). Being human affords us many ways to understand and express our human existence. I teach racially and ethnically diverse groups of learners. What is needed for their minds and bodies is not separate and apart from what is needed to edify their souls, the deepest parts of who they are as humans. I am oriented as a member of the human race who believes my African ancestors paved the way for my existence. Shared legacies and African cultural dimensions (Boutte et al., 2017) are evident in my life and my work with students. These include spirituality (not religion), harmony, verve, communalism, affect, oral tradition, improvisation, and perseverance. I engage in this work through the lens of *ubuntu*. Ubuntu, "I am because we are," as it is a relational worldview that originated from the Zulu people on the continent of Africa. Botho/ubuntu was foundational in southern Africa and demonstrates how, historically, interconnectedness and interdependence have been valued throughout the continent and the African diaspora.

It Truly Takes a Village

Children come into our learning spaces as whole beings. Families and their "village" of kinfolk and community members are their child's first teachers. Families teach children the languages of their hearts, minds, and spirits. They are the first conveyors of culture, both directly and indirectly. Embracing and loving Blackness is demonstrated when we, as educators, respect the ways Blackness is embodied by our students and their families including ways of speaking, hairstyles, dances, and other forms of expression as well as the ways they make meaning of the world.

Centering children and their families has always been a key consideration when preparing during the first weeks of the school year and continuing throughout the remainder of the year. As I enter my empty classrooms as a prekindergarten, kindergarten, 1st-, and 2nd-grade teacher, finding a prominent place to feature students and their families is important. Each year, I construct a 3D paper family tree in a place in full view within the classroom. As I meet students and their families, whether at back-to-school night or the first day of school, I photograph them (with their families' permission) for our class family tree. Added to the photograph is a QR code. I add the photos to the family tree as well as to their desks or cubbies. The QR code allows families to access and share their family photos with others. Families also send additional photos throughout the year as they add photos of extended family members and special events. Starting in 2017, the Adinkra symbols for interconnectedness and learning from the past have been displayed with the photos to reinforce the connections of students to their families and families to our class and the class to our connected histories. The beauty and diversity of the Black family are on full display.

Africanize It!

There is power in our children embracing, understanding, and honoring the brilliance, creativity, resistance, and resilience of Black people throughout time and space. After my 2017 4-week experience in Cameroon, West Africa, my teaching was transformed. I began to Africanize everything as my teaching became more Africancentric. We studied Africa and ourselves as members of the African diaspora. For the next 4 years after visiting Cameroon, I taught 3 years in 1st grade and 1 year in 2nd grade. Following those 3 years, I taught 2 years of African studies for all students enrolled in kindergarten through 5th grades; about 400 of those students were in grades kindergarten through 3rd.

Ubuntu—I Am Because We Are

Each year my goal is to create a space where students know that they were important, irreplaceable members of our classroom family. Great importance is placed on honoring the humanity of each member of our class family. Posted in my 1st- and 2nd-grade classes was ubuntu, "I am because we are." From the first day of the school year through the last, our focus was on how we could exist as one ensuring that every member of our class was loved and respected. We defined what respect looked like in our classroom space using a Pro-Black worldview and acknowledging that not all cultures define and demonstrate respect in the same ways. Our classroom interactions were guided by Ubuntu and the values represented by Adinkra symbols (see Figure 5.1). We discussed and interpreted our schoolwide expectations as well as civic dispositions through the use of Adinkra symbols and values. The four schoolwide expectations included: (1) Respect all people and property; (2) Solve problems peacefully; (3) Be responsible for your learning; and (4) Demonstrate appropriate behavior at all times. For each of our four schoolwide expectations, we used an Adinkra symbol as the visual representation of that expectation. For example, children selected an Adinkra symbol for interconnectedness for the expectation, of *respecting all people and property* as shown in Figure 5.1.

Figure 5.1. Classroom Poster of the School Expectations and the Matching Adinkra Symbol

This process required us to think carefully about how we defined respect and to refrain from framing respect using Eurocentric norms (i.e., speaking only when spoken to, only raising hand to speak and be recognized, only using standardized English), which promote hegemonic practices that perpetuate anti-Blackness. We oriented respect using ancestral knowledge, drawing on the principle of ubuntu. I recognized that by doing this, the classroom environment was more in sync with who our students were, where they presently and historically came from, and the ways in which we wanted them to exist in time and space.

Throughout our time together, we continued to discuss the civic dispositions of *respect, compassion, cooperation, honesty,* and *empathy* and why the development of these dispositions was important to a society in which each person was affirmed and treated fairly. The classes and I identified a corresponding Adinkra symbol for each civic disposition and made signs to display around the room. Using this ancestral knowledge of key principles and values served as the cornerstone of our classroom culture. Our classes engaged in a communal approach where collective decision-making was valued and each member's humanity was considered and honored.

Akwaaba—Welcome!

I was taught at a young age to always warmly acknowledge and greet anyone with whom I came in contact. In Black culture, greetings are incredibly important and are a way of honoring the presence of others around us. Whether it's a verbal greeting, head nod, handshake, big hug with a few pats on the back, a warm embrace, or a fist bump, acknowledging others is important. While visiting West Africa, the power of greetings was on full display. One of the first sights after arriving in Ghana was the greeting *Akwaaba*, meaning "you are welcome," painted on billboards, on walls, and filling the air as we entered a variety of spaces. In Nigeria, there were endless ways to greet others depending on the time of day, the age and community status of the person or people present, and the level of formality required.

I utilized this Black cultural knowledge when greeting my young students and encouraging them to greet each other. Before entering the classroom, I offered each of them a hug, high five, fist bump, or wave. Many students demonstrated their creativity and brilliance,

Figure 5.2. Morning Meeting Welcome Slide With Learning Songs

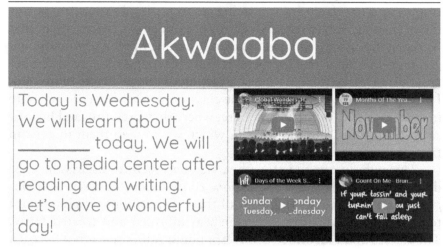

verve, and expressive individualism, and started offering their own creative greetings that I was honored to fully embrace. During our morning community meetings, we continued to welcome each other with Akwaaba as well as songs and dances using a song (video) like *Global Wonders Hello Sing-Along* (2008), which utilized other greetings from around the world as shown on the learning slide in Figure 5.2. The greeting of Akwaaba became a mainstay in my work with young children.

AFFIRMATIONS: POSITIVE MESSAGES

"I am a sweet daughter.
I am sunshine from the sky.
I am sunlight in my eyes.
I am myself.
I love my family.
I am a thoughtful person."

—Affirmations by Savannah (pseudonym), 2nd-grader, 2022-2023

Savannah's affirmations beautifully state how positively she feels about herself and how connected she is to others. Affirmations and an affirming environment are critical to having a Pro-Black learning space. There is great power in these positive messages. I used affirmations and affirming messages throughout the learning process and engagements with my students. I introduced the students to writing affirmations in 2022 using a video of an affirmation song by JOOLS TV, *Affirmations: JOOLS TV Trapery Rhymes* (2022). This affirmation song epitomizes Pro-Blackness—the beats, the rhymes, the message, and the visuals. The lyrics reinforce loving one's skin and hair as well as never giving up and being kind and strong.

Like Savannah, other children used the song as inspiration for writing their affirmations. Children used their creativity, brilliance, and connectedness to write about themselves in Pro-Black ways. Each class started with the children reading their affirmations to themselves and adding affirmations as they felt inspired. Children eventually created a personal book of affirmations adding Adinkra symbols that represented the affirming message on each page.

Another powerful resource was the affirmations poem "Who Am I?" by Ronnette Brown Curls (Pink Thumb, 2021). This poem draws on the power of ancestral knowledge and connectedness paired with meaningful visuals. It affirms students' identities, intelligence, creativity, and strength. The students recited this poem after reading their affirmations.

The class's structures, processes, and learning experiences must affirm who students are to embrace Pro-Blackness truly. We must not just use affirmation poems or songs at the start of the day, then allow everything else we do throughout the day to be disaffirming. Affirming environments represent Black love, pride, and joy.

Representation of all kinds is essential. The lyrics of the "Affirmations" song by JOOLS TV (2022) state, "I love myself. I love my skin. I love my hair, my melanin." Pro-Black learning spaces embrace the beauty of every skin tone, including the darkest of hues, which is in direct opposition to the Western beauty standards, which privilege skin tones identified as White or closer to White. When students entered the room, they saw the beauty and diversity of their family photos and African art, as shown in Figure 5.3.

Students created self-portraits using skin-colored crayons and construction paper. I encouraged them to match the crayons and paper with their skin tone by comparing each to their skin to find the corresponding color, as shown in Figures 5.4a and 5.4b. Giving the students time to do this is key.

Figure 5.3. African/Ghanaian Painting Displayed in Classroom

Figures 5.4a and 5.4b. Kindergarten Students Finding Matching Crayons for Self Portrait

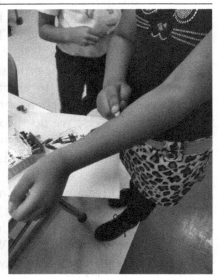

Our classroom community roles were Africanized, a shift away from my approach from earlier years. I made a personalized badge for each student as shown in Figure 5.5. The badge included each student's photo, name, our school, and the Adinkra symbol for *interconnectedness*. I wanted their names and images to be included

Figure 5.5. Classroom Jobs Student Badge

because, as stated previously, representation in many forms matters. There was a variety of roles. The following provides a brief description of two Africanized roles.

Instead of a line leader, we had a *Keeper of the Walking Stick*. This student walks in the front of the class carrying a walking stick. The role was symbolic of leaders and warriors who would go ahead of others to ensure the path was safe and appropriate. There were other roles as well. Instead of the role of *Caboose* at the end of the line, we had the role of *Keeper of the Classroom*. As the Keeper of the Classroom, the student would be the last to leave the classroom, ensuring all classmates had exited the room and closed the door. This role did not replace adult supervision. Rather, it served in a role of shared responsibility to ensure all classmates were accounted for and reinforcing Ubuntu, I am because we are.

Answering to the Beat of the Drum

I introduced the students to African dance and its connection to traditional and contemporary dances from Africa and the African diaspora. A community elder, who taught community-based African dance classes, taught a session for all 1st-grade students. This served as the students' formal introduction to African dance. We incorporated African dance and my novice playing of the djembe (drum) into our schedules, regularly using video tutorials such as the *Five(ish) Minute Dance Lesson—African Dance: Lesson 3* (2012a). In subsequent years, I coupled African dance with two videos about the origins, making, and uses of the djembe drum, *Five(ish) Minute Drum Lesson—African Drumming: Lesson 1: The Djembe* (2012b) and *Djembe—Making a Djembe—Ghana, West Africa* (2008). It was important for students to broaden their understanding of the drum's history and deepen their knowledge of how our ancestors created and used the djembe.

Each subsequent year I expanded the numbers and styles of dance taught, always focusing on authenticity and connectedness to the Black experience. Over a 2-year period, students learned more than eight African dances from different geographic and cultural groups in Africa. These included Nigeria's Bino and Fino *Dance, Dance, Dance* (2019), Ghana's Blacktown Arts' *Drumming Workshop for Kids: Learn African Dance Steps to "A Lion Has a Tail"* (2020), South Africa's *Ndlovu Youth Choir—Jerusalema Dance Challenge* (2020), and Dance N' Culture's *Dance for Kids! African* (2021). Dances from throughout the African diaspora were included as well including *Dance for Kids! | Hip Hop* (2021b) from the United States and the Cumbia dance using Zumba® *Latin Easy-to-Follow Basic Steps Tutorial for Beginners* (2022) from Colombia, South America. At the culmination of our dance sessions, we engaged in single nasal breathing or other forms of deep breathing allowing us to reduce our heart rates, center ourselves, and connect to our ancestral roots while utilizing the Black cultural dimensions of spirituality, harmony, verve, and movement.

As a part of our Harlem unit, the students viewed and learned the dance the Harlem Shake and tried their best ballet moves as a video of the Dance Theatre of Harlem's dancers illuminated the screen. They were able to see Black bodies moving with varying energy and verve. The Harlem unit was not the first time the students saw ballet through a pro-Black lens. Earlier in the school year, they learned about a group of Black fathers who were featured by the *Philadelphia Tribune* (2019). These Philadelphian dads accompanied their daughters, with both their presence and their ballet moves, to weekly ballet classes. This provided an affirming view of the Black family and countered some of the misconceptions about Black fathers' involvement with their children and who can and cannot enjoy ballet.

Standin' on the Shoulders of Our Foremothers and Forefathers

Africans' early and continued contributions to mathematics, science, the arts, and the world's cultures were integrated across content areas. The children studied, wrote, and read about freedom fighter Nelson Mandela, President and lawyer Barack and First Lady and lawyer Michelle Obama, legendary athlete and entrepreneur Serena Williams, scientist and astronaut Mae Jemison, mathematician Katherine Johnson, scientist and scholar George Washington Carver, inventor Lewis Howard Latimer, inventor and entrepreneur Madame C. J. Walker, mathematician and Global Positioning System (GPS) cofounder Gladys West, and so many others.

I carefully curated learning songs and videos to support their content exploration and skill development. More importantly, I wanted their content to be culturally affirming and pro-Black.

The exploration of their content was intentionally interdisciplinary. They were (and are) living social studies. They were the embodiment of history. The students used their skills as readers, writers, listeners, and speakers as they engaged with each other and a variety of content in meaningful ways.

One example of an extended learning experience with my 2nd-grade students occurred during the 2020–2021 school year. My 2nd-graders and I engaged in an ongoing inquiry unit called From *His*tory to *Her*story and *Our*story. I recognized the importance of finding ways to provide mirrors (affirmations of students' cultures) and windows (perspectives beyond students' worldviews). I wanted students to know that historians are diverse, and I focused specifically on illuminating the experiences of women and people of color as historians.

South Carolina's social studies standards focus on themes to help students develop skills to become historians and geographers. We used an integrated approach to study history, geography, economics, civics, and government. This way, we learned about current and past events in the United States and the impact of Blacks' creativity, brilliance, resistance, and resilience on these events. Students learned to view history as a vibrant, inclusive, and relative topic. The Adinkra symbol of the sankofa bird, which symbolizes learning from our collective history as we move forward to the future, was used to anchor the learning.

The class discussed how different people and groups might view and understand events. These viewpoints, preferences, and agendas privilege some events and experiences and discount or omit others often excluding or distorting the contributions of Black people. Throughout the history unit, our focus was to include events in history that allowed students to see people whose lived experiences are/were similar to their own and who had/have a more nuanced life than is commonly reported. Also, it was important for students to learn about those whose lived experiences may be/have been different than what is included in typical narratives. The Adinkra symbol for interconnectedness was identified due to the interconnected nature of historical events and Black people throughout history. Children illustrated events in their lives that were important, unusual, and interesting before moving into the development of a class timeline.

At the start of the unit, I introduced the blank timeline, as shown in Figure 5.6. We discussed how timelines could be used to

Figure 5.6. The Blank Timeline

Africanizing the Early Childhood Curriculum

Figure 5.7. The Developed Timeline

organize historical events by dates and themes (including *her*stories and *our*stories).

Our timeline was organized by decades, starting in 1960 and continuing through the present. The timeline started with the date 1960 because of the integration of the New Orleans public school system by Ruby Bridges, as shown in Figure 5.7.

Children identified with Ruby Bridges, who was a young Black child. Students also have included important people in their lives who were born in 1960 and after. The unit was anchored with the students and their lives; our local school and community leaders; as well as national and international figures such as trailblazer Ruby Bridges,

Vice President Kamala Harris, activist Maya Angelou, and National Youth Poet Laureate Amanda Gorman, who all used their creativity, brilliance, resistance, and resilience to make a difference in the lives of Black people and the world.

The first events added to the timeline were the children's and my birthdays and photos. It was important for our timeline to be anchored by the students so that they know they are an important part of history and to see their Black and brown faces in a place of prominence, as shown in Figure 5.8.

During Week 2, the class used a variety of sources to identify the lives of American figures, many of whom identified as Black—some whose lives were well documented, others whose lives are lesser known but just as important, unusual, and interesting. Some of the

Figure 5.8. Timelime With Children's and Teacher's Birthdays

Figure 5.9. Student Work Selecting Civic Dispositions

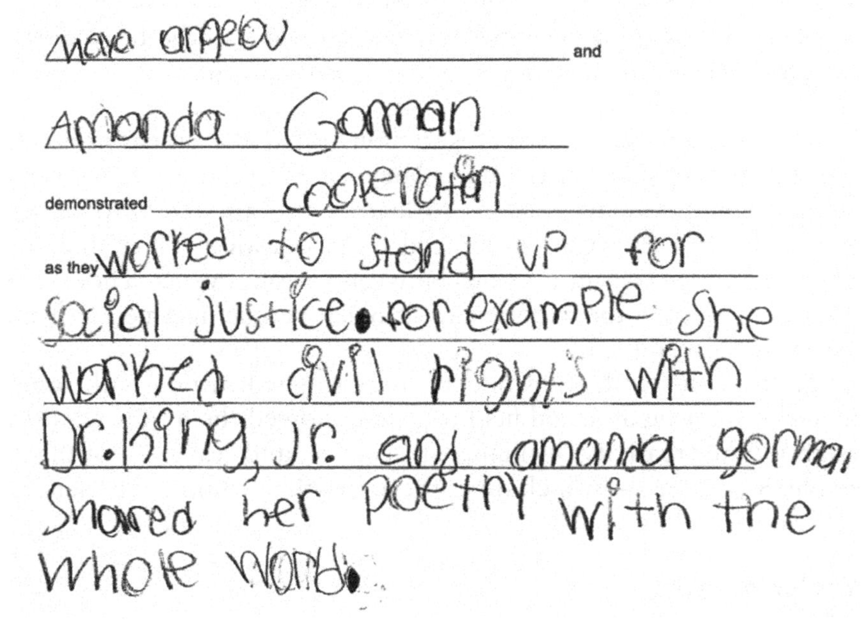

> Maya Angelou _____ and
> Amanda Gorman _____
> demonstrated ___ cooperation ___
> as they worked to stand up for
> social justice. for example she
> worked civil rights with
> Dr. King, Jr. and amanda gorman
> Shared her poetry with the
> whole world.

figures featured included Nikki Haley, our state's female governor; Steve Benjamin, the first African American mayor of Columbia, South Carolina; and my dad, Mr. Titus Duren, a member of one of the first classes of graduates to integrate Clemson University who later held leadership positions in a variety of community and educational spaces.

During one task of the unit, the students selected two individuals of personal, community, state, or national significance and noted what civic dispositions the selected individuals have exhibited in their lives, as shown in Figure 5.9. The Adinkra symbol for cooperation was the force of this period of instruction.

The following vignette illustrates what the students have learned during this period of instruction. Madison (pseudonym) walked in one morning and recounted her interaction with her mother the night before.

> "Ms. Collins, last night I asked my mom some questions. I asked her if she was the only Black child in her school and she said, 'No.' I asked her

if she was treated unfairly at school and she said, 'No.' I asked her what year she was born and she said, '1981.' May I add this to the timeline?" Madison proceeded to get two adhesive notes and added the data she collected from her interview with her mother to the timeline.

Madison and her classmates demonstrated the emerging skills of historians throughout the unit. They asked questions. They used primary and secondary sources to learn more about Black people throughout history. And then asked more questions. The students compared and made connections between various events. They were able to understand the experiences of Black people in America from 1960 through the present.

By the unit's end, the students shared their learning with other classes by offering a virtual field trip that allowed them to teach others about the creativity, brilliance, resistance, and resilience of Black people. Several classes, including one at another school, experienced the field trip.

W Is for Wangari

> "[Dr. Wangari] helped her community by planting trees and she got into good trouble."
>
> —Malaysia, kindergarten student, 2023

During the 2021–2022 and 2022–2023 school years, the children explored the lives of people who, in John Lewis's words concerning working on behalf of justice, got into "good trouble." One of the people we discussed was Dr. Wangari Maathai, mother, environmentalist, activist, and founder of the Kenyan Greenbelt Movement. Our study of her life focused on her care for and dedication to her Kenyan community. During the unit (see Figure 5.10), we utilized print and online resources including the book *Wangari's Trees of Peace* (2008).

Dr. Wangari's life was a consistent example of the dimension of harmony. She witnessed the destruction of her beloved community in the name of development and progress. After returning from her studies abroad, she found deforestation and its negative impacts being experienced by her neighbors. The trees and many of the animals were gone. The women were having to carry firewood long distances. She decided immediate action was needed.

Figure 5.10. Kindergarten Student's Drawing of Doctor Wangari Maathai

Dr. Wangari's life demonstrated communal focus and the importance of cooperative economics. She trained and employed thousands of women in an effort to plant millions of trees across Kenya. Her commitment was unwavering even as she was threatened, assaulted, and jailed by police in an effort to deter her from continuing the work to restore trees removed by deforestation.

Throughout the unit, kindergarten and 1st-grade children made many connections and expressed new learning. They were able to empathize with Dr. Wangari and her people. Children were able to identify the importance and uses of trees from their own experiences and other learning. They expressed how much courage it took for Dr. Wangari to stand up even as she and others were being threatened and mistreated. They connected the good trouble of Dr. Wangari to others we studied such as Rosa Parks and Queen Mother Nana Yaa Asantewaa of the Ashanti (Asante) people of West

Africa. Each child created an alphabet page and added the sentence "Ww is for Wangari" as an extension of their learning. A picture, as shown in Figure 5.10, was drawn representing their remembrance of Dr. Wangari's work.

CONCLUSION

As early childhood educators, we must ensure that Pro-Blackness is centered in our learning spaces. This requires us to first examine our beliefs about Blackness and to intentionally make pedagogical decisions that develop our children's literacy about the African diaspora. We must remember an important part of understanding Blackness is knowing that there is great diversity in the Black experience. While there are shared histories, there is diversity in the contemporary and historical experiences of Black people. So as Early Childhood educators, as we approach how we shape the learning environment, we must be careful to avoid perpetuating stereotypes and not allow anti-Black practices to make their way into our classroom sphere. An affirming classroom is not reductive. It is one where the Black love, joy, creativity, brilliance, resistance, and resilience of our young learners is present and celebrated.

CHAPTER 6

Pro-Blackness as a Loving Antidote in Early Childhood Classrooms

Janice R. Baines

Jamal (7-year-old Black child): Ms. Baines, I know why teachers say African American.
Ms. Baines: Hmm . . . tell me about it.
Child: Well, it's nicer than saying, you know, Black.

I paused and recalled an incident in the hallway where the word Black was used derogatorily during a transition time between related arts classes. Several classes were in the hallway when a student shouted, "Get your ole Black self out of my way." The other student responded with, "I ain't Black, with yo' ugly, Black self." Their teacher, rushing to get the students to their destination, reprimanded them with a shush and entered their classroom. To respect the request of the administration, the remaining classes retreated to their related arts classrooms. After returning from related arts and then to class, a student asked me if I was Black. I proudly said, "I'm Black, and I am proud! Yes, I am Black." When I identified myself as Black, the children gasped. It was apparent that they had not embraced their Blackness and viewed Black as negative. I also thought about the lack of language used throughout the school community to elevate Black children's identity and questioned myself. Was I doing enough, and how had I consciously tried to show Pro-Blackness beyond words?

INTRODUCTION: EXPLORING WHAT PRO-BLACKNESS MEANS IN EARLY CHILDHOOD CLASSROOMS

Pro-Blackness in Early Childhood refers to an intentional effort to promote and celebrate Blackness and Black culture in the classroom (Boutte & Compton-Lilly, 2022). It involves creating a learning environment that affirms and values Black children's experiences, histories, and perspectives. Pro-Blackness also commits to dismantling systemic racism and promoting social justice in education. I have observed how incorporating Pro-Blackness in Early Childhood curriculum can significantly impact Black children's self-esteem, identity, academic success, and sense of belonging (Bishop, 1990).

I reiterate that Pro-Blackness does not mean excluding or marginalizing other cultural groups in this context (Boutte et al., 2021a). Instead, it emphasizes recognizing and celebrating the diversity of experiences and cultures within a classroom. It also creates a space where all children can feel seen and valued. Ultimately, incorporating Pro-Blackness in early childhood classrooms is a critical step toward creating a more equitable and inclusive education system for all children.

HEALING THROUGH LEARNING: THE POWER OF PRO-BLACKNESS

"Oshe! Oh-she-oh! Oshe Baba!"

(Wherever you go, you can always come home to love.)

—Traditional Ghanaian song

My experience with understanding and developing a love for my Black identity differs from Jamal's (in the opening scenario). Growing up, I always felt connected to my African heritage. My family shared our history in bits, and I longed to understand more about where I came from as I developed my own identity. At the core of that identity is Blackness. Coupled with family history, my family ensured I was fully immersed in Black culture by reading authors such as Virginia Hamilton, Sharon Draper, and Walter Dean Myers. This foundational preparation sparked the need to continue to research Blackness, including African history and culture.

When I was a relatively new teacher, I attended a roundtable discussion hosted by the Center for the Education and Equity of African American Children (CEEAAS). At that roundtable, I was introduced to the power and possibilities of Black children through an Africancentric lens. This experience began my journey of re-membering (King & Swartz, 2014) my histories and knowledges, some of which had been sidelined during my teacher preparation program. Re-membering, as discussed in Chapter 1, refers to reassembling parts of Black culture that have been underutilized not only by educators but by Black people in general. Re-membering is an ongoing source of healing for Black people. My re-membering included learning about the experiences of people of African descent around the world to help me feel more connected to my cultural heritage (King & Swartz, 2018) and to give me a sense of belonging to the African family. Boutte et al. (2017) refer to this process as African diaspora literacy.

Despite this newfound (recovered) knowledge, I still felt unease and disconnection from being African. I yearned to experience African culture firsthand and see where my ancestors called home. That's when I received an invitation to a Fulbright-Hays travel grant to Ghana. Although this was not my first trip to the "motherland,"[1] it was the first time that I had a plan. My plan was to use what I learned to make my teaching more Pro-Black.

As soon as I stepped off the plane, I was struck by the vibrant colors, the lively music, and the welcoming people. The words "Akwaaba!" welcomed me like a mother's embrace. A new world was shown, drenched in Blackness. Over the course of my trip, I visited historical sites such as Cape Coast and Elmina Slave Dungeons. This is where enslaved Africans were held captive before being sent to the Americas. I also visited Kwame Nkrumah Memorial Park, honoring Ghana's first president after independence and pan-Africanist leader. But the most transformative experience was visiting the W. E. B. Du Bois Center in Accra, Ghana. These experiences gave me a deeper understanding of the European transatlantic slave trade and its impact on African people and their descendants worldwide. I also connected with local Ghanaians, participated in cultural ceremonies, and enjoyed traditional Ghanaian foods.

What was most meaningful for me was the healing feeling I experienced. Being in Ghana allowed me to see African culture's beauty and resilience and to embrace my identity as an African descendant. I felt a sense of belonging and connection I had never experienced before. Before the trip, I had completed my time in one school district and was transitioning to another. During this time, I experienced a major loss of having my mother become an ancestor. That shattered

Figure 6.1. W.E.B. Du Bois Center in Accra, Ghana, 2018

my being, and I was lost. So, the experience in Ghana was particularly profound, healing, and transformative for me. I also venerated my beloved mother as we honored Dr. W. E. B. Du Bois in his mausoleum (Figure 6.1).

Learning about African diaspora literacy was just the beginning of my journey toward healing and self-discovery. My trip to Ghana helped me find peace and connection to my cultural heritage.

In this chapter, we will cover several topics. First, we will discuss how African diaspora literacy can shape the classroom and create a warm environment. Next, we will explore how the physical features of the classroom can be used to create a unique decor. We will also discuss the importance of showing love to students on their first day of class. Additionally, we will delve into the history of Black people using sankofa as a toolbox. Finally, we will look into the future of

Pro-Blackness in early childhood classrooms. This chapter is a love letter to change agents, those ready to transform education. I share my journey of creating a space of love.

PRO-BLACKNESS: SHAPING THE CLASSROOM WITH AFRICAN DIASPORA LITERACY

Black magic, black excellence
Black habits, this black medicine, everything
Black *Chucks, black tux, everything*, everything
Black *hug, black love, everything*

—Smoke, 2020

After my transformative trip to Ghana, I knew I wanted to share my knowledge with my students. As a teacher, I felt responsible for ensuring that my students deeply understood African history and culture. I wanted to create a space where they could feel proud of their Blackness. I wanted my students to embody what I had learned through experiencing African diaspora literacies in the making. I thank Dr. Gloria Swindler Boutte for exposing me to the conversations that led to this ideology.

As noted in Chapter 1, Dr. Gloria Swindler Boutte coined the term *African diaspora literacy* to refer to the collective knowledge, experiences, and perspectives of those displaced from their African ancestral homelands (Johnson et al., 2018). It provides a framework for understanding how African peoples' shared history, culture, and language have been maintained and passed down through generations despite displacement from their homelands. By understanding this concept, we can gain insight into the unique challenges faced by people of African descent in different parts of the world and how they respond to them.

Children in classrooms that center on ADL develop an understanding of the complex histories and experiences of people of African descent around the world. By becoming literate about the African diaspora, Black children also develop a sense of agency and empowerment. They learn to use their own voices to speak out against racism and discrimination, and they become active participants in the fight for racial justice and equity.

In classrooms where students respond to African diaspora literacy, teachers are fostering a deeper understanding and appreciation of the African diaspora and helping to build a more inclusive and equitable society. They are creating spaces where diversity and representation are celebrated, and students are empowered to become agents of change in their communities and beyond.

To integrate ADLs into my 2nd-grade classroom, I began by incorporating books, films, and art showcasing African culture's diversity. I introduced my students to music, Ghanaian children's literature, and Kehinde Wiley's artwork, among many others. We also studied African history, from the ancient empires of Mali and Ghana to the Civil Rights Movement struggles in America. We also discussed the challenges and struggles that Black people have faced throughout history and today. Throughout history, I always emphasized Black people's resilience, strength, and creativity (Wynter-Hoyte & Smith, 2020).[2]

I knew that teaching about African culture was not enough. I wanted to create a space where my students could feel proud of their Blackness and see themselves represented in the curriculum (Baines et al., 2018). So, I worked to create a classroom environment that celebrated diversity and embraced different cultural perspectives. We had open discussions about race, identity, belonging, and representation, and I encouraged my students to share their own experiences and perspectives.

Besides teaching about African culture and history, I also created opportunities for my students to express themselves creatively and explore their own identities through poetry and artwork. I encouraged my students to be proud of their Blackness and to see themselves as valuable contributors to our society.

As I saw my students engage with the material and embrace their cultural heritage, I felt a sense of fulfilment and purpose. The knowledge and experiences I gained in Ghana made a difference in their lives. They saw themselves as part of a global community, connected to a rich cultural heritage, and proud of their Blackness.

In the end, integrating ADLs into my classroom was not just about teaching history or culture. It was about creating a safe space where my students could feel seen, heard, and valued. It was about empowering them to embrace their identities and see themselves as agents of change in a world that often fails to recognize their worth. And it all began with my journey of healing in Ghana.

FROM THE WINDOWS TO THE WALLS: AFRICAN DIASPORIC DECOR

When I returned from Ghana, I was a 2nd-grade teacher who was passionate about creating a classroom environment to inspire and empower my students. I knew that many of the children in my classroom were Black, and I wanted to make sure they felt proud of their identities and cultural heritage (Boutte et al., 2021a).

To achieve this goal, I decided to decorate my classroom with positive images of Black people. I started by putting up posters of Black leaders, innovators, and artists such as Malcolm X, the Obamas, and Oprah Winfrey. I also included images of Black children playing, reading, and exploring the world around them (see Figures 6.2a, 6.2b, and 6.2c).

Figures 6.2a, 6.2b, and 6.2c. Malcolm X and Silhouettes; African American Imagery; Positive Black Images on Wall

Figures 6.2a, 6.2b, and 6.2c. *(continued)*

As I put up the posters and arranged the decorations, I felt a sense of excitement and anticipation. I knew my students would be excited to see themselves represented in the classroom, and I hoped that the positive images would help to reinforce a positive sense of identity and self-worth. When the students arrived on the first day of school, they were amazed by the transformation of the classroom. They eagerly pointed out the posters and decorations, and I could see the pride and excitement in their eyes. I knew I had made the right decision in creating a space that celebrated their cultural heritage and identity.

Throughout the year, I continued to use posters and decorations to reinforce positive messages about being Black. I would point to the posters and tell my students stories about the accomplishments and contributions of Black people throughout history. I encouraged them to see themselves as capable, talented, and valuable members of society. As the school year came to a close, I reflected on the decorations' impact on my students. I could see the confidence and pride that they had developed throughout the year and knew that the positive images had played a role in shaping their sense of identity and self-worth.

Decorating my classroom with positive Black images was not just about creating a visually appealing space. It was about creating a space that celebrated diversity, embraced different cultural perspectives, and empowered my students to be proud of who they are. And it was clear that I had succeeded in achieving that goal.

AKOMA: A PROCLAMATION OF LOVE

I was always passionate about creating a welcoming and empowering classroom for my Black students. I was always on the lookout for ways to incorporate Black culture and history into my curriculum and to help children develop a sense of pride and empowerment in their own identities. My goal was not only to make them feel pride but to make them feel loved and welcomed.

While preparing for school one day, I came across "These Three Words" by Stevie Wonder (1991). The song's lyrics spoke to me, conveying love, hope, and resilience. It would be the perfect way to introduce children to the concept of love, but also a way to engage them. I started by playing the song for the children and encouraging them to listen closely to the lyrics. I explained that it was written by Stevie Wonder, a legendary African American musician, and celebrated Black love and unity. I asked the children what the lyrics meant as they listened to the song. I encouraged them to share their thoughts and feelings and discuss how the song related to their experiences.

Children were engaged and excited and enthusiastically shared their thoughts and feelings. They talked about how the song made them proud of their Blackness and gave them hope for a brighter future. They also talked about how the song reminded them that they were not alone.

I incorporated "These Three Words" into my lessons, using it as a jumping-off point to explore the history and culture of the African American community. I then paired the song with an introduction to Adinkra symbols. I introduced *akoma*, the Adinkra symbol that means "heart" (see Figure 6.3). It is a powerful symbol of love and unity in Akan culture. I used it as a foundation for teaching classroom rules and expectations that can effectively convey the importance of love and respect in the classroom.

Figure 6.3. *Akoma*, the Adinkra Symbol That Means "Heart"

I explained the significance of akoma in Akan culture. I made clear that love is not just something to say but also an action that requires respect, kindness, and consideration for others. Using the akoma symbol as a visual aid, we created a set of classroom rules that promote a culture of love and respect. For example, the symbol encouraged children to:

- Speak and act kindly toward each other.
- Listen to each other's opinions and ideas.
- Respect each other's personal space and belongings.
- Help each other when needed.
- Take responsibility for their actions and words.

The symbol reinforced positive behavior in the classroom. For example, a small heart-shaped token or sticker with the akoma symbol on it can be used to reward children who demonstrate acts of kindness and respect. They will not only learn something about Akan culture, but also how to show love and respect to others through their actions and words.

In my classroom, the akoma became a badge of honor. Children helped each other with their homework, offered words of encouragement during difficult times, and even made small gestures of kindness, such as sharing a snack or a toy.

SANKOFA: MORE THAN BLACK HISTORY

Dr. Joyce King, a prominent educator and scholar, has long advocated for teaching students about their histories and cultures. At a conference, she stressed the need for students to be exposed to different historical perspectives and approaches to gain a comprehensive understanding of the past. Dr. King explained that many students are only taught a narrow, Eurocentric view of history that focuses primarily on White people's achievements and perspectives. This limited view can damage students, particularly those from marginalized communities, as it leads to feelings of disconnection and alienation from their own cultural heritage.

To address this issue, Dr. King emphasized the importance of exposing students to a wide range of historical perspectives and approaches. This could include studying the history and contributions of different cultural groups. It could also include exploring the intersections of race, gender, and class in history, and examining how power and privilege have shaped historical narratives.

I decided to create a unit on the Adinkra symbol sankofa, which represented learning from the past to move forward. I wanted to take Dr. King's advice for students to see history in different ways, and to understand how their own experiences were connected to the broader historical context.

For their first assignment, I asked children in my class to interview Black faculty and staff members at their school. We learned about stories and how to write them to lead children in this direction. We examined many biographies and autobiographies, especially of historical figures. Children summarized what they had learned about the person. They even transferred their learnings about the Adinkra symbols to the person's characteristics.

Interviewees (teachers and staff at the school) were asked to tell the children how they lived their lives as Blacks. They were also asked why they chose to teach and who and what kept them inspired. Children were engaged with the lives of the people with whom they had daily encounters. This helped them see the school as more than just a place to learn, but as a community—a community of people who loved being Black.

As a new year began, I was excited about building on successes like the sankofa assignment. Little did I know that in the middle of the year, we would be catapulted into a COVID pandemic and would be teaching online. This required rethinking ways to engage children and maintain Pro-Black and vervistic approaches. I was determined to find new and innovative ways to teach students during the pandemic. One day, I decided to teach them how to conduct interviews, even though they were learning from home. I knew that interviews could be a powerful tool for learning, allowing students to connect with experts in different fields and gain valuable insights into different perspectives. I also knew that conducting interviews could be a valuable skill for children to learn, as it would help them build their communication and critical thinking skills.

I decided to use a combination of technology and hands-on practice to teach them how to conduct interviews during the pandemic. I started by teaching them about the different types of interviews, including informational interviews and research interviews. Next, I showed them how to use videoconferencing tools like Zoom and

Google Meet to conduct virtual interviews. I also had them practice interviews with their family members and friends, using the skills they learned to prepare and ask follow-up questions.

Finally, I had them conduct interviews with experts in different fields. The students were tasked with asking them about their personal experiences with discrimination and racism, and how they had overcome those challenges. The goal was to help the students see how the struggles of the past were still present in their own community. I invited guest speakers to join their virtual class sessions and allowed the students to ask them questions about their experiences and perspectives. The students were surprised by what they learned. They discovered that many of their teachers and staff members had faced discrimination and racism in their own lives but had persevered and succeeded in spite of those challenges.

By the end of the unit, the students had a new appreciation for the importance of understanding history in order to create a better future. They also interviewed and wrote biographies for community members as seen in Figures 6.4a and 6.4b. They realized that the

Figures 6.4a and 6.4b. Biography About Community Member

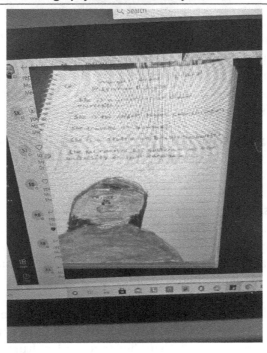

Figures 6.4a and 6.4b. *(continued)*

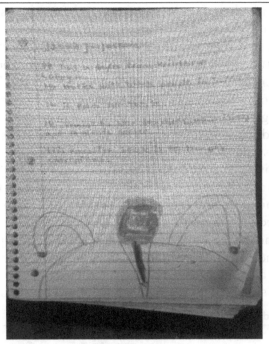

struggles of the past were still present in their own lives but that they had the power to overcome those challenges and create a better world for themselves and others. They felt a sense of pride in their own cultural heritage and were inspired to continue learning about Black people's histories and cultures worldwide.

CONCLUSION: THE FUTURE OF PRO-BLACKNESS IN EC CLASSROOMS

Child: Ms. Baines.
Ms. Baines: Yes.
Child: I know why "Dear"[3] isn't coming today.
Me: Oh really, tell me about it.
Child: Because she will teach people how to love students like us. Black students. Black people.

Early Childhood educators can promote positive racial identity development as part of Pro-Black strategies. The goal is to help Black children become proud of their heritage and cultural identity and develop a positive sense of self (Wynter-Hoyte & Smith, 2020). A variety of methods can be used to accomplish this, including exposing children to diverse books, music, and art that reflect Black culture as well as providing opportunities for them to share their own cultural traditions.

Pro-Blackness in Early Childhood classrooms should also promote social justice and equity. This involves teaching children about the experiences of Black people throughout history and exposing them to current social justice movements and issues that affect the Black community (Broughton, 2022). This can help them to develop empathy, understanding, and a sense of responsibility for creating a more just and equitable society.

A more diverse and inclusive learning environment is also essential for the future of Pro-Blackness in Early Childhood classrooms. The curriculum should reflect the diverse experiences of all children, regardless of race or ethnicity, and promote diversity in the classroom by hiring more Black educators (Boutte & Bryan, 2019). Embracing Pro-Blackness in Early Childhood Education can help all children have a brighter future regardless of their background or identity.

CHAPTER 7

African American Language (AAL)
It's *the* Language for Me

Gloria Swindler Boutte

A popular phrase in Black culture is, "It's the __ (fill in the blank) for me." This connotes that the named thing is compelling in some way. The phrase can be used as a compliment or an insult (don't you just love the flexibility of Black language? I do!). An example is below.

A Black woman walks in the room with a hairstyle that is fire (translation: alluring). Two Black women in the room look at her in admiration. One woman says, "It's the hair for me!" (compliment)

For this chapter, I use the phrase "It's the language for me" to convey two points. The first point is captured by Dr. Toni Morrison's comment about African American Language (AAL), and I dare not add anything to that.

> The language, only the language.... It's a love, a passion. Its function is like a preacher's: to make you stand up out of your seat, make you lose yourself and hear yourself. The worst of all possible things that could happen would be to lose that language.... It's terrible to think that a child with five different present tenses comes to school to be faced with books that are less than his own language. And then to be told things about his language, which is him, that are sometimes permanently damaging.... This is a really cruel fallout of racism.
> —Toni Morrison, as cited in Alim & Smitherman, 2012, p. 167

The second point is complementary to the first. Here, I emphasize the word *me*. *It's the language for ME*. I recast the phrase to mean that AAL is *the* language for Black people. That is, it is the quintessential language. AAL is our mother tongue, and the first language of 80–90% of African American people in the United States (Dillard,

1972). It is the language *for* me/us! It is the language in which we can be our most authentic selves. It shows up in our music, our poetry, our writing, our pain, and our joy. It is the "language we cry in" (nod to a documentary, *The Language You Cry In,* 1998), and it is the language we rejoice in. In Pro-Black settings, it should be embellished, amplified, and respected—and never relegated to a lower-status position.

When I am teaching and/or during professional development on African American Language, I can anticipate that most people have never learned that AAL is a complete rule-governed language system. In fact, it is one of the most sophisticated and distinct variations of English in the United States. It has five verb tenses and linguistic characteristics that other languages can only dream of—for example, the *habitual be* (look it up). Yet I cannot count the number of times Black educators and friends have shared the trauma they faced as a child when using African American Language. Indeed, they are so traumatized that they have done an excellent job of continuing the tradition of traumatizing others. Once I teach them the linguistic features of AAL, it is often liberating.

A main point is that early in life, young AAL speakers are taught that their language is "broken" and not good enough. I assure you that Black children's language is not broken and neither are they.

My mother taught the four of us to use Standardized English (SE), and it was not until my siblings and I started studying AAL more than four decades ago that I came to realize her goal. Understanding that AAL was marginalized in schools and society, she perceived SE as ammunition against the endemic racism that we faced in school and society. I am sure she was taught to devalue AAL by teachers with good intent as well. But as April Baker-Bell and others have noted, "I can switch my language, but I can't switch my skin" (Baker-Bell, 2017). And like it or not, what people think of AAL has more to do with what they think of Black people than the language (which is structurally and linguistically rich). And using SE will not prevent discrimination. This is not to say that Black children should not add SE to their linguistic repertoire, but they should not do it in ways that devalue AAL.

We used AAL freely, as did my mother, in daily conversations with family and friends. It pains me still to see that Black children are taught early on to dismiss AAL and to distance ourselves from it (with the hopes of "succeeding" in life). From a Pro-Black perspective, nothing could be further from the truth. Signithia Fordham (1988) rightly pointed out that when Black children have to downplay their race and assume a raceless persona, it is a Pyrrhic victory in that it is a goal achieved at too great a cost. Anything that alienates children from their families and culture is problematic. Language has the dual purpose of being both a means of communication and a carrier of culture (Ngugi Wa Thiong'o [1981]). Language and culture are interrelated, and loss of one results in the loss of the other (Sharma, 2019). In Pro-Black classrooms, cultural excellence is just as important as academic excellence. Children cannot be culturally excellent if they are detached from their culture.

What we do during the Early Childhood years can have a long-lasting impact if not redirected. My mother is now 87 years old and has been diagnosed with early dementia. Short-term memory seems to be most affected, and much of her long-term memory is still intact. Deep in the memory is an indelible distaste and intolerance for AAL—though she and I like to use it jokingly. The director of the senior center she attended relayed the following story to me about my mother. The context is informal, and there are about 10 senior citizens who regularly attend the program. My mother is one of three African Americans. I conveyed to the director that one goal I see for my mother is for her not to shrink and become less agentive than her regular sassy self. Chuckling, the director explained, you do not have to worry about that. She is *very* outspoken. The director elaborated. . . .

> The other day one of the Black men said, *I is.* . . . Before he could complete his sentence, she (my mother) interrupted and said, "You IS nothing. You ARE a Black man and you need to speak properly." The Black man complained that my mother was attacking him. I told him that your mother is a Black woman who had to work hard and has a lot of respect and dignity.

Of course, I do not judge parents (and my mom) because we know what we know. As parents (and teachers), we do the best we can. As Maya Angelou once said, "Do the best you can until you know better. Then when you know better, do better" (Good Reads, 2023).

My hope is that this chapter will encourage EC teachers to respect and honor AAL in their classrooms. So this chapter is a cautionary tale of sorts. I remind teachers not to lose the larger goal of keeping

Black children's spirits intact when aiming for the narrow goals of "success" based on Eurocentric definitions. The approach(es) used to help AAL speakers add on SE make all the difference in the world. Some approaches can be classified as linguistic violence or attack on children's home language (Boutte & Bryan, 2021). The linguistic assaults are often done in full view of other children, thus teaching SE speakers to also devalue and disrespect AAL.

LOVING, RESPECTING, AND HONORING AAL

I have written extensively elsewhere on the features of AAL (phonology, syntax, morphology, semantics, and pragmatics) as well as linguistic strategies for teachers and schools (Boutte, 2013; 2015b; Boutte et al., 2021a; Boutte & Baker-Bell, 2022; Boutte & Johnson, 2013a, b), so I will not recount AAL features here. In the remaining sections, I provide three key points to guide teachers' journey of learning to love, honor, and respect AAL in EC classrooms: (1) learn by listening to AAL speakers, (2) use AAL-friendly policies and assessments, and (3) update classroom resources to include mirrors for AAL speakers.

Learn by Listening to AAL Speakers

And the children shall lead. . . . Teachers should position themselves as learners and notice linguistic patterns that AAL speakers use. These are not mistakes as children's language follows linguistic rules. For example, using the previous use of the verb *is,* suppose AAL speakers regularly say, "I is. You is. We is. They is," and so forth. The consistent use of *is* represents a pattern. In AAL, the linguistic rules allow the verb *to be* to remain constant regardless of person (regularization). So there could be a million people and the verb would still be *is*. This is totally *correct* using AAL syntax. The child is speaking AAL—not SE. See Boutte (2015) and Boutte & Johnson (2013a, b) for strategies for honoring AAL and adding SE to promote biliteracy (SE and AAL).

AAL should be viewed as a co-parallel language (Boutte, 2016; 2022), not as an *inferior* language or a language relegated to informal speech and settings. What young children learn early on about AAL can make the difference between whether they love or detest the language. This means that teachers have to educate themselves instead of engaging in linguistic attacks that can devastate children and alienate them from their home language and culture. Children should not have to choose one language over the other.

Use AAL-Friendly Policies and Assessments

Many language assessments position AAL as *incorrect* English (see Boutte et al., 2021, and Boutte & Baker-Bell, 2022, for detailed discussion and recommendations). Here again, once teachers become aware that Black children enter classrooms as whole people who have a viable and sophisticated language that they have used to communicate effectively, they (teachers) will need to examine assessments using a critical Pro-Black lens. It is recommended that EC educators engage in ongoing professional development so that they can examine policies to see if they are AAL-friendly.

Many/most language assessments do not distinguish between language delays, disorders, and AAL, and Black children's language is misdiagnosed. For example, AAL speakers do not distinguish between many homophones such as *pen* and *pin*. On auditory tests, their pronunciation, then, is often marked wrong. Hence, an AAL-friendly policy would require that the person doing the assessment speaks or understands AAL phonological rules. Likewise, AAL lexicons (semantics) are different than SE. So, if AAL speakers are asked to point to a picture of a toboggan, for instance, and they do not have that word in their lexicon but know it by another name, they would be judged as not knowing the object. Perhaps it is just called a hat in their lexicon.

We know that AAL speakers are interrupted when reading aloud at much higher rates than SE speakers for perceived miscues. This interferes with reading fluency and likely children's perceptions of themselves as readers. AAL speakers receive ongoing covert and overt messages that there is something wrong with the language, which translates that there is something wrong with them, their families, their communities, and their race. This is all done in the name of teaching reading. Adding insult to injury, AAL speakers rarely, if ever, see their language in books and other media used in school.

Update Classroom Resources to Include Mirrors for AAL Speakers

When children do not hear or see AAL in the curriculum, they get the message that it is unimportant and inferior—not worthy of being in a classroom. This is something teachers can change immediately by adding AAL books, videos, and other resources. One caveat is that non-AAL speakers will benefit from using read alouds from *Sankofa Read Alouds* on YouTube or having an AAL speaker record the books. My concern here is that the reading should be authentic and should not sound as if AAL is being mocked or as if it is a *foreign language* that is difficult to speak.

A sampling of books that provide positive affirmations of AAL are listed below.

Notice the intentionality in the text set of using both boys and girls, urban and rural settings, and historical and contemporary times to demonstrate the elasticity and dynamic nature of AAL.

1. Battle-Lavert, G. (1994). *The barber's cutting edge.* Children's Book Press. AAL syntax and semantics are on proud display in this book as a boy engages in dialogue with the barber in a barbershop. The narrative captures sentences without linking verbs ("What you got up your sleeve today, my man") and double negative—both of which are permitted in AAL linguistic rules. Note the figurative language that AAL speakers excel in and that teachers can and should build on. Also, pay attention to the cultural familiarity (communalism) through the use of the phrase *my man*.
2. Cooke, T. (1997). *So much.* Candlewick Press. This book features a contemporary family's birthday party for a dad. The baby is the center of attention, and everyone who enters the house greets the child first—highlighting the love of a Black child in families. Morphological examples such as "The daddy rub the baby face" can be detected by astute AAL investigative teachers.
3. Duncan, A. F. (1995). *Willie Jerome.* Macmillan Books for Young Readers. From the title of the book and throughout the narrative, Black culture and language shine. Filled with communal love, rhythm, oral traditions, and movement, this

story about a young boy playing jazz on the rooftop in a city sizzles. Readers can enjoy hearing AAL syntax ("She don't wanna hear his noise"), semantics, phonology, morphology, and pragmatics.
4. Smalls, I. (2003). *Don't say ain't*. Charlesbridge Publishing. Features a young girl in an urban city who learns to be biliterate (speak both AAL and SE).
5. McKissack, P. (1986). *Flossie and the fox*. Penguin. This historical fiction folktale is set in the rural South and features a young girl outsmarting a fox. The girl, Flossie, speaks in AAL and the fox speaks in SE. Phonological, syntactic, semantic, and pragmatic language examples can be found throughout. For instance, Flossie refers to her grandmother as *Big Mama*, which does not refer to her physical size but is symbolic of her significance to the Black family. Flossie uses the AAL pragmatic rule of "communicating impressively" as she uses her sassy language to outsmart the fox as he uses SE.
6. Rosales, M. B. (1996). *'Twas the night before Christmas*. Cartwheel Books. This book has great examples of AAL phonology that demonstrate that ending and medial sounds may be omitted (e.g., *short'nin'* for *shortening*). The communal nature of Black culture is also beautifully captured through the depiction of a Black family.

CONCLUSION

In Pro-Black classrooms, teachers honor African American Language. This is a formidable mission since it is routinely disrespected in instruction, curriculum, policies, assessment, and daily commentary. Likewise, Black people and their language are disrespected in the media and society as a whole. Regrettably, this has positioned far too many teachers (even Black teachers) in the role of policing children's language. Helping Black children have healthy understanding of the power of their language is key.

I should note that just because children and families use the language does not mean that they realize it is a legitimate, rule-governed language system. This is where Pro-Black teachers can play an important role of not only educating themselves about AAL but also helping Black children understand that *It is the language for them.* Many EC teachers may not have been aware that AAL is not *broken* English and that it *is* a rule-governed language. I end with a popular African American saying, "And if you don't know, now you know!"

CHAPTER 8

What's Up, Fam (Family)?

Saudah N. Collins and Jarvais J. Jackson

> During my (Saudah) almost three decades of teaching, I have encountered families with great love and care for their children. Even my students from challenging situations usually had a broader village who was there to love and support them through tough times. I experience so much joy when years later we meet again and they tell me of the fond recollections they have of our time together.

We do not teach children in isolation, disconnected from their families. If our classrooms reflect our students and their families, then we have done something right. If our students feel the love and care that is reflected within their homes and communities, then we have done something right. This chapter features family and community engagement in Saudah N. Collins's K–5 African studies class. It also includes examples of family and community engagement from a 1st-grade teacher (before she begins teaching African studies). It is coauthored by Saudah N. Collins and Jarvais J. Jackson since Jarvais also collected data on her classroom during his 3-month case study of her classroom (see Chapter 4). We include voices of Saudah and her family members as they reflect on family–school connections. Examples and larger themes can be easily extrapolated to other EC settings, though we focus on K–3 experiences in this chapter.

SAUDAH'S COMMENTARY

To embrace Pro-Blackness is to embrace the Black family and community. My goal is to celebrate the diversity of the Black family while focusing on love, joy, connectedness, creativity, and brilliance. As a Black mother, daughter, sister, aunt, educator, and friend, I bring my Blackness into my teaching. That is not to say teachers who do not identify as Black cannot be effective, caring, knowledgeable teachers who embrace Pro-Blackness and the Black family.

EXISTING WITHIN UBUNTU

I am because we are.[1] I am the teacher. I exist because of my biological and extended family. So, when I think of the ways in which I engage with my students' families and communities, it mirrors my experiences with my own family. During my 27 years as an Early Childhood educator, I have drawn on familial, personal, and professional relationships to offer my students perspectives from Black communities locally, nationally, and globally. For example, my sister, Tahirah, has played a crucial role in my development of African diaspora literacy. She is well versed in many areas and is a powerful resource. Tahirah shared her expertise in using plants to dye fabrics with my kindergarten children. Drawing on processes used by our ancestors, she taught the children how to dye cotton fabrics using purple cabbage and turmeric. They were fully engaged as they were able to learn about this dyeing process while using all their senses and making connections to ways our ancestors were in harmony with nature. EC teachers can draw on familial and community connections (like Tahirah) when planning classroom activities.

Second-graders interviewed my dad as a part of the historical study unit described in Chapter 5. They studied his life and developed interview questions. The interview experience was not only enriching for the children but for my dad as well. He appreciated their thoughtful questions and inquiry into his life as a Black educator and community leader. Engaging family members helps children view me beyond the walls of the classroom. They understand that, like them, I am also a member of a family.

The following examples involve two of my children. My son, Goler, while in college, volunteered in my 1st- and 2nd-grade classrooms. He read with students and supported them as writers and mathematicians as shown in Figure 8.1. Goler shared about his studies at a Historically Black University.

My daughter, Ameerah, volunteered to choreograph and teach a dance to a group of 3rd-grade girls after school. The dance, to

Figure 8.1. Goler Working With a Student

a song about Harriet Tubman's courageous efforts to lead the enslaved to freedom, was performed for my school's annual Black History program.

BLACK FAMILIES ARE DYNAMIC AND DIVERSE

Black families are dynamic. We are diverse in our configurations, lifestyles, belief systems, experiences, and other ways in which we engage within the world. I have taught students from military families; varying socioeconomic backgrounds; those who primarily lived with a single parent, grandparent, or other relatives; as well as students who lived in blended families or with two parents. Some of my students have lived in foster care or experienced homelessness. Each family has its own story. Each family was honored and welcomed.

Connecting with families and the community is an essential part of creating Pro-Black spaces for our children. Students should see their families represented within the classroom. As discussed in Chapter 5, photographs taken of the families at school as well as family photographs from home are wonderful ways for students to be able to see their family's presence in their learning space daily. They also get to see the families of their classmates.

Children also saw themselves represented through community materials included throughout the room as featured in Figure 8.2. We displayed various community restaurant menus as well as family recipes. We also included the *Black Pages*, a local publication featuring

Figure 8.2. Community Materials Displayed in the Classroom

Black business owners and other professionals, as well as a newspaper that featured many positive events and citizen recognitions as well as concerns in the local Black community.

One year my 2nd-grade students completed a project entitled *My Family, My Culture*. I created a slide presentation template that the children and their parents could modify as desired. For children who needed a higher level of support and needed to complete their project at school, I assisted them with the project's completion. They added photos and videos representing important aspects of their culture, including hairstyles (Afros, braids, ponytails, and temp fades) languages (African American Language, patois, and standardized American English); dances; clothing; and foods. They presented their projects to the class. When one child included a slide and stated his favorite dance was the Electric Slide, many of his classmates were unaware of the dance. So we scheduled a time when he and his mother could teach the class the dance virtually. The class learned the Electric Slide and thoroughly enjoyed learning it from their friend and his mother.

HONORING AND UNDERSTANDING BLACK FAMILIES

As educators, it is important that we view families as more than just the suppliers of extra snacks and chaperones for field trips. We must find ways to create an ongoing dialogue and be receptive to feedback. We must honor varying communication styles and understand that there is a lot to be learned from families. We are the professionals in the classroom and facilitators of learning, but we also must understand that there are additional bodies of knowledge and literacies among families.

Occasionally, I have experienced pushback. Some families have expressed concerns possibly due to the ways that we have been educated related to racialized identities, African American Language, and countering dominant Western perspectives. When concerns arise, I refrain from being defensive and attempt to create a meaningful dialogue over time. Once a parent expressed concern about her child discussing skin color as he sang a song about loving oneself. I called to discuss how and why we were discussing skin color. The parent's concern was alleviated after more information was provided as to how this song was a positive song that we used to learn to love and appreciate aspects of ourselves as well as others.

Figure 8.3. Meet Thaddeus IV and His Family

I met Thaddeus IV and his family (Figure 8.3) during his 1st-grade year and as his mother joined our teaching team. At this time, I was teaching 1st grade and not African studies. Thaddeus was bright and very talkative around his family, but very quiet when he entered the classroom. About his 1st-grade start, his mother wrote:

> After moving to a new city, I met Ms. Collins at my new job. I'd heard how amazing of a teacher she was and was honored to have her as my son's first-grade teacher. My son had not always liked school and

What's Up, Fam (Family)?

definitely did not like new surroundings. With this, moving to a new school in a new city was not going to be the easiest experience. If it weren't for Ms. Collins then I really don't think we would've had a positive first-grade experience.

During our first several days of school, Thaddeus did not say very much to me or his classmates. He enjoyed drawing. His first sight word assessment yielded zero responses. I took a photo of his sight word assessment and uploaded it to SeeSaw, a web-based platform that connected schools and families. Families can see uploaded videos, photos, and other creative work of the students within seconds of them being posted. Those who elected to link to the children's accounts could view, like, and comment on each post. Families loved it and so did the children! It was a great two-way communication tool.

Each year, at least 80% of children's families linked to the students' accounts. Thaddeus's family linked and commented (as shown in Figure 8.4). Concerning his sight word assessment, his mother wrote, "I hope he builds the courage to read for you the next time. ♡" I responded, "He will. When I give him a little time and space, he joins us. ♡" Thaddeus's father wrote, "He will be ready for you next time."

Figure 8.4. Sight Word SeeSaw Entry With Family and Teacher Comments

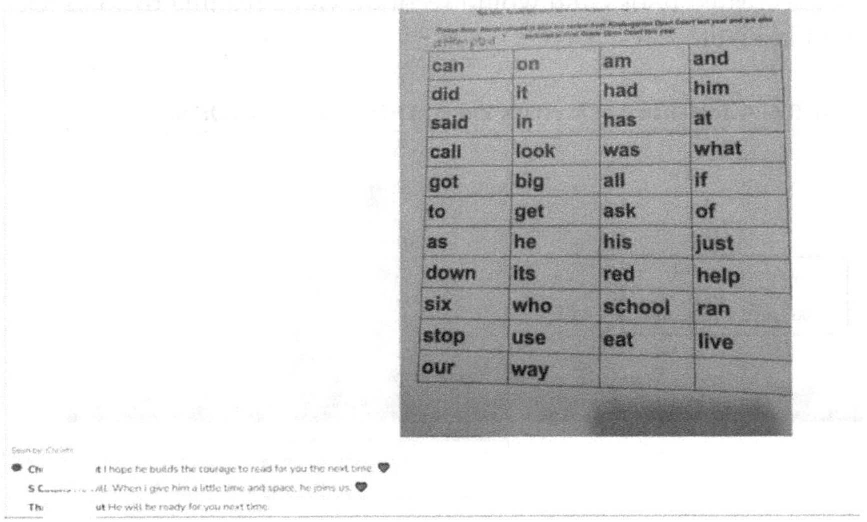

can	on	am	and
did	it	had	him
said	in	has	at
call	look	was	what
got	big	all	if
to	get	ask	of
as	he	his	just
down	its	red	help
six	who	school	ran
stop	use	eat	live
our	way		

- Ch: It I hope he builds the courage to read for you the next time. ♡
- S C......: ...ll. When I give him a little time and space, he joins us. ♡
- Th: ...ut He will be ready for you next time.

Figure 8.5. Myson Sharing His Work

I believe in the knowledge and learning abilities of every Black child, Thaddeus included. I was not going to make assumptions about him nor was I going to give up on him. I knew that by keeping his family informed, they would be able to continue to support his growth as well.

As the year continued, Thaddeus became more comfortable in our classroom space. He continued to enjoy drawing and willingly engaged in the life of the classroom. Thaddeus uploaded his work throughout the day (see Figure 8.5).

He created books and would record a video reading them as featured in Figure 8.6.

Figure 8.6. A Screenshot of Myson's Video of Him Reading His Original Work

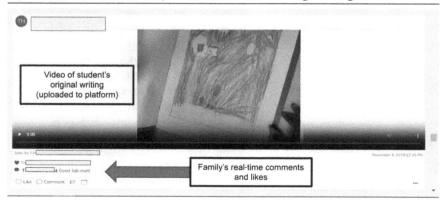

Figure 8.7. Myson's Dad Blowing Out Candles

His family continued to be actively engaged as well, regularly liking and commenting on his uploads. While studying light, Thaddeus's family accepted my invitation to upload photos of light and shadows in their world away from school as shown in Figures 8.7 and 8.8.

Thaddeus finished the year feeling confident as a reader, writer, and mathematician. It took a true partnership between his family and me. Since his 1st-grade year, I have had the pleasure of teaching Thaddeus for two years in African studies.

His mother offered additional reflections about Thaddeus's journey. She wrote,

> When in her class, I slowly observed my son's view on school shift from being uninterested to becoming excited to share what he learned in class. The thing was, he shared about the instruction he was receiving that reflected Culturally Relevant Pedagogy (CRP). He was happy to share about himself as a black boy as well as about his classmates of different heritages. This showed the culturally competent component of CRP.

Figure 8.8. Myson Found His Shadow Before Bed

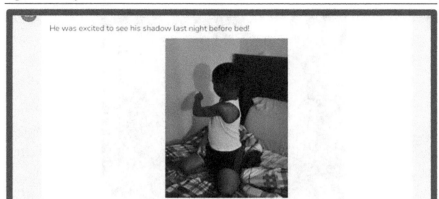

He was displaying a *windows and mirrors* mindset as he appreciated his own culture as well as respected and appreciated the culture of his friends in his class. He became excited about going to school to learn more about Africa and the brilliance of the beautiful continent.

His 1st-grade year was when COVID-19 surfaced and changed our everyday lives. It also was the summer of the racial injustice done to George Floyd. My son was able to understand what was going on and identify that black lives truly matter and that something had to be done about all of the racial injustices going on around him. He would dress up in a suit and would set up a play podium made from a cardboard box saying he was the president and that he would change the things that were happening. This showed another component of CRP, critical consciousness. These speeches built his confidence and allowed for him to improve his speech (which he struggled with) and writing skills. His writing and reading comprehension also improved. These experiences were when my son was in first grade. He is now in third grade and has grown even more in love with African studies as well as learning about different cultures around the world. As a parent and educator, my children being happy is and always has been one of my greatest desires. Seeing my son go from despising school to loving it is one of the best feelings I could ever ask for.

My goal is for every family to have that feeling of knowing their child is growing and developing in an environment that values them. My students come to me with varying levels of support. I ensure I make every effort to connect with families as partners and that students know our learning space is a place where their Black love, joy, connectedness, creativity, and brilliance are embraced and truly valued.

JARVAIS'S COMMENTARY—AFRICAN STUDIES OVERVIEW: AKWAABA MEANS WELCOME

During the year 2017, Ms. Collins had her first experience on the continent of Africa during a study abroad project. From that year forward, she centered the role of Africa, Africans, and African Americans in her teaching. The following year, she traveled to Ghana[2] and continued to deepen her knowledge and experiential base on African studies.

Ms. Collins was overjoyed about being asked to teach students about African history as she says, *all day, every day*. She viewed this as a way to transform curricula that typically excluded African and African American histories. During the development of the course, she drew from her experiences in Cameroon and Ghana and spent a great deal of time researching the continent of Africa and the African diaspora, acknowledging that she still had much to learn. While always an outstanding teacher, the new African studies content revitalized Ms. Collins, who had been teaching for three decades.

Beyond a litany of small details about Africa and African-descendant people, Ms. Collins focuses on deep African values that can be reiterated across the year in all grade levels and content areas. For example, early in the year, Ms. Collins introduced civic dispositions of respect, honesty, compassion, empathy, and cooperation using Adinkra symbols. Students designed name tents and folders to identify important values to them, their families, and the community (Jackson et al., 2021). They also used Adinkra symbols as a tool to analyze characters in text and lyrics in music.

Thinking about the global African community, Ms. Collins began the year by introducing Africa as the *mother continent*.

Using the name *Alkebulan,* she explained that this was the continent's name given by its people. While many people hold narrowly stereotypical views about Africa (e.g., lots of poor, hungry people; governmental corruption), children in Ms. Collins's class often express a desire to visit or live in Africa after hearing agentive, Africancentric perspectives. They often excitedly share what they learn with their families, thus extending the influence of the African studies course beyond the classroom. Below I highlight insights from three parents from my 3-month research in Ms. Collins's African studies classroom. I selected these since one represents a White parent, one is both a teacher and parent, and one is Africancentric.

HEARING AND HONORING FAMILIES' VOICES

"African studies has become a conversation piece at our house . . . they want to know so much."

—A. Cash, personal communication, February 23, 2022

At the beginning of this school year in 2021, families received a survey to share their initial thoughts about the new African studies class. Results showed that 92% of families *agreed* or *strongly agreed* that the African studies class was essential. The opening quote is from an interview with one of many family members who have expressed gratitude for the implementation of African studies. Ms. Cash, a White parent with multiracial children, shared that the African studies course inspired her family to learn more about the children's Black background and culture. Ms. Cash and other parents expressed confidence in Ms. Collins's ability to teach the class. Ms. Cash explained, "I was mainly excited because I know what type of teacher [Ms. Collins] is, and I know what the kids will actually get from [Ms. Collins] being the one who is teaching." Ms. Cash shared that her son refers to Africa as "mom's house." His excitement sparked her interest in learning more so that she could support her children's learning at home. Many parents echoed Ms. Cash's sentiments in the survey, admitting that they would enjoy learning more themselves.

THERE IS HOPE—REFLECTIONS OF
MS. CHRISTINA STOUT, TEACHER

"I was sleeping all those years, and I am so excited my children are able to learn."

—C. Stout, personal communication, April 26, 2022

Ms. Christina Stout represents the perspective of a teacher and a parent. As the mother of two JCES students (1st and 3rd grades), she stressed gratitude that her children are learning about who they are and what they come from as Black people. She reflected on the absence of Black histories in her upbringing. As a military child, Ms. Stout experienced schooling in a few states. She learned rudimentary elements of Black histories, including a romanticized rendition of enslavement and of figures such as Martin Luther King and Rosa Parks but nothing about Africa. Stating this was a period of being asleep, Ms. Stout says that the African studies course has sparked her interest in having more conversations at home about African and Black histories and culture and including it with her instruction as a kindergarten teacher.

Ms. Stout's 1st-grade son has come home and thrown "African parties" where he shares what he learned in class, including the songs and dances. Ms. Stout vividly remembers a day they looked up Black figures together and her son stated, "I am the future Black president." This excitement for school and learning is in stark contrast to his earlier experiences in school. Before coming to Ms. Collins's class, her son did not enjoy school, and she struggled with ways to piqué his interest. By no means did coming to Ms. Collins's class change all of the difficulties with school for her son, but she began to see a tremendous change in how he engaged with learning. She credits African studies for some of this renaissance, explaining that seeing his transformation gave her *hope*.

Ms. Stout's daughter, a 1st-grader, brings home similar excitement about the content learned in African studies. While her daughter doesn't throw African parties, she makes connections to everyday life, such as when watching television or seeing billboards while driving. Ms. Stout recalls a moment when her daughter saw Amanda Gorman on TV. She went into an entire lesson teaching the family what she learned about Amanda in African studies. Ms. Stout acknowledged that the ongoing references from both her son and daughter are refreshing as she only learned about the negative sides of Blackness in school. The class has inspired her as a parent to do more research with her children. She is a firm supporter of African studies, stating,

> If we just teach our children now to not stereotype, if we teach them the beauty and the brilliance of Africa, and how Blacks shouldn't just be looked at in a negative light; if we teach them all that how to accept everybody and just love on everybody; . . . if we teach them that now, just imagine the world that we live in. (C. Stout, personal communication, April 26, 2022)

CONTINUING THE LEGACY—REFLECTIONS OF MS. KEDA DUBARD

Ms. Keda DuBard spent her early years adorned in African fabrics. She and her family wore them so much that they were featured in the local newspaper, and many assumed they were from Africa. Her family was heavily engaged in African and African American culture and history throughout her life and has tried to bequeath that same knowledge to her 1st-grade son, who attends the school. Ms. DuBard explained that she was thrilled to hear that there would be an African studies class as it would complement what she was doing at home. Like Ms. Stout, she said that the course gave her hope. She was encouraged that the school decided to implement this class even amid the current climate. She was honored that her child would be getting some context about his experience in America.

Ms. DuBard hoped that other families would receive the course as she did, hoping this could be the blueprint for other schools. She emphasized the importance of engaging in cultures, especially Black culture as it is often overlooked. She reflected on raising a Black boy in America, saying,

> Here in America, it hits a little different. I would love for him to grow up in a world where [race] is not an issue, not a concern [where] he doesn't have to constantly rework how he fits into society. However, that's not currently the fact of the matter. And so, I worry that no matter

how much I can tell him, he's amazing, and other people can tell him, he's amazing; who he is, [is] a little brown boy—that he won't see that reflected in the media, and other aspects beyond ones who care about him. And so, with this class, I hope that it's just another source of information that he can use to build who he is and details I might not think to bring to him. (K. DuBard, personal communication, April 26, 2022)

While her son does not have strong opinions as a 6-year-old, Ms. DuBard finds joy in hearing his retelling of content taught in school. She states that he more readily offers information about African studies over any other subject. His remarks on the kings and queens of Africa, such as Mansa Musa, have generated conversations at home and encouraged further research. He is also eager to show off the dances and songs learned in the class. Ms. DuBard stresses her faith in the school, Ms. Collins, and the content in African studies. She hopes that her son can apply these concepts to his life and use this knowledge to conceptualize his life. Ms. DuBard says, best of all, it's free information.

CONCLUSION

As evidenced from the examples, Saudah's class is a wonderful model for other EC teachers who wish to engage families and communities regarding the use of Pro-Black content and pedagogies. Saudah communicates with families in person and virtually. Two-way communication between families is the norm as well as her focus on academics and other matters. Communications are informal and formal but always authentic. Saudah keeps families connected to local and global Black events. There is an open invitation for families to visit the classroom, volunteer, and to find out what's up. Likewise, Saudah routinely reaches out to see what's going on with families and finds ways to integrate family realities into her classroom. She does not only ask families to share their lives, but she shares hers as well. Overall, Black families express a deep appreciation to Saudah for ensuring that their children feel validated in the classroom. This is the essence of Pro-Black family relationships.

CHAPTER 9

Reimagining Classroom "Management" Using Pro-Black and Restorative Approaches

Jarvais J. Jackson

One day in class, after Justin (3rd-grader) continued to show what is typically considered misbehaving (i.e., wearing a hood, talking out, and talking back), I took him to my desk to have a chat with him about his behavior. I asked a simple question: "What is going on?" His response felt as if I had opened a floodgate that needed relief. Asking that question was the first step into understanding what was happening in Justin's mind and world that resulted in his behaviors in my class. Our conversation became a moment where he could confide in me about things that seemed minute to adults but were rocking his little world. We worked out goals and a plan together, and his behavior positively improved from that moment. Later, he wrote in a note to me, "You are the first teacher who just listened to me." Those words will forever stick with me and guide how I think about classroom management. This was one of the pivotal moments in which I understood that classroom management was bigger than rules, and it was truly about building healthy relationships.

For decades, the academic literature has been crystal clear that Black students are disproportionately over-disciplined, leading to disproportionate suspension and expulsion rates beginning in preschool (Milner et al., 2018). While there is enough literature and untold stories to write myriad volumes on this issue, this chapter focuses on what can be done as we seek liberation from oppressive systems.

Readers who are unfamiliar with the body of literature will find it helpful to read scholarship such as ones listed below.

- Anderson, M. D. (2015). Why are so many preschoolers getting suspended. *The Atlantic.*
- Gregory, A., & Roberts, G. (2017). Teacher beliefs and the overrepresentation of Black students in classroom discipline. *Theory Into Practice, 56*(3), 187–194.
- Hines, E. M., Ford, D. Y., Fletcher Jr., E. C., & Moore III, J. L. (2022). All eyez on me: Disproportionality, disciplined, and disregarded while Black. *Theory Into Practice, 61*(3), 288–299.
- Howard, T. C. (2019). *Why race and culture matter in schools: Closing the achievement gap in America's classrooms.* Teachers College Press.
- Milner IV, H. R., Cunningham, H. B., Delale-O'Connor, L., & Kestenberg, E. G. (2018). *"These kids are out of control": Why we must reimagine "classroom management" for equity.* Corwin Press.
- Monroe, C. R. (2005). Understanding the discipline gap through a cultural lens: Implications for the education of African American students. *Intercultural Education, 16*(4), 317–330.

When I present on classroom management, I start with three definitions without providing the words that they define; (1) the process of *dealing* with or *controlling* things or people, (2) *determining* the behavior or supervising the running of, and (3) keeping the surroundings or conditions in which a person, animal, or plant lives or operates in good condition or in working order by checking or repairing it regularly. I give participants, often teachers, a chance to ponder and see if they can figure out what words are being defined. Following the moment to think about what words these definitions might be defining, I provide participants with a slide that matches the words with the definitions (Figure 9.1).

I start with this to problematize the idea of classroom *management*. When thinking of managing something, it often takes away the humanity of the person involved. It suggests that the person is not capable of thinking or contributing to the larger group without being

Figure 9.1. Slide Defining Classroom Manaagement

Management

the process of **dealing** with or **controlling** things or people

Control

determining the behavior or supervising the running of

Maintenance + Environment

keeping the surroundings or conditions in which a person, animal, or plant lives or operates in good condition or in working order by checking or repairing it regularly.

told what to do or how to do it. I use this to begin interrogating the idea of the words we use to describe what we are doing. Is it our goal to *control* every action of our students and create disciplinary action for when they are "not in line," or are we trying to create a safe space for students to learn and grow as people socially, emotionally, and academically? While the sheer volume of literature on classroom management highlights its significance, the critical question arises: *What is being done for Black students as a counteractant to the harm that is being done to Black students in classrooms across the United States* (Johnson et al., 2019)?

Black students are victims of many types of anti-Blackness within schools. Johnson et al. (2019) provide five types of anti-Black violence in schools: (1) physical, (2) symbolic, (3) linguistic, (4) curricular and pedagogical, and (5) systemic. All five types of violence show up in schoolwide expectations and procedures and subsequently classroom expectations and procedures. Classroom "management" strategies are often exclusive of Black students' cultures, voices, and ways of being. While the literature is substantial in discussing the problem, I draw attention to solutions as a remedy to the harm done to Black students.

In this chapter, I challenge readers to think about the semantics of classroom management and push toward the idea of creating a classroom community where teachers are facilitators *and* members of the class, and children are also members who play a vital role in the community. I emphasize that teachers are members of the community. Who teachers are as humans is an essential part of the community, so the classroom should not simply be focused on them as the singular members of the community who deserve to be happy and comfortable. Like any community, the needs, desires, and comfort of all members should be considered. All members of the community should be affirmed. Communities in each classroom and from year to year will look and feel different since members of the community change and so will the needs. Yet, at the core, the goal is to build and maintain an inclusive community.

In the following sections, I unpack classroom communities and their purpose. I comment on the body of literature on the topic and share background on African value systems that can be established in lieu of typical rules. I provide a few exemplary examples of teachers with flourishing Pro-Black classroom communities.

BACK TO OUR ROOTS, COMMUNALISM

"I am because we are, and since we are therefore I am."

—South African proverb (ubuntu)

I use the idea of community when describing what I see as liberating classrooms. In Chapter 2, readers were introduced to the *Black cultural dimensions* (Boykin, 1994). Throughout this chapter, I will both explicitly and parenthetically refer to these dimensions in ways to build and maintain community. For a foundational understanding of why I accentuate the concept of community, I bring focus to the communalism dimension. Boykin (1994) refers to communalism as "a commitment to the fundamental interdependence of people and to social bonds and relationships" (p. 249.) African people, from the beginning of humanity, have been communal people and have prioritized community (Maphalala, 2017; Venter, 2004). Even with this fact, because of colonialism, self-focused individualism has become the norm, even accepted by some Black people (Boykin, 1994). Boykin et al. (1997) argue that communalism within cooperative learning spaces results in high-caliber student performance—the goal for all students.

At the beginning of this section, I shared a South African proverb known as ubuntu. Ubuntu (mentioned in several chapters in this book), commonly explained as *I am because we are,* highlights the African thought of communalism. Venter (2004) defines ubuntu as a "philosophy that promotes the common good of society and includes humanness as an essential element of human growth" (p. 149). Ubuntu offers two themes that will continue to show up throughout the chapter, as both are essential to achieving Pro-Black classrooms: community and humanness. President Obama eloquently explained the embodiment of ubuntu during a memorial service for South African president Nelson Mandela:

> There is a word in South Africa—Ubuntu . . . a word that captures Mandela's greatest gift: his recognition that we are all bound together in ways that are invisible to the eye; that there is a oneness to humanity; that we achieve ourselves by sharing ourselves with others, and caring for those around us. (Obama, 2013)

The emphasis on humanness is important as Black children have been dehumanized in schools for decades. This dehumanization deprives them of basic protections, and subsequently, they receive harsh(er) treatment (Goff et al., 2014). Further, dehumanization strips the dreams and autonomy to be and think from children (Legette et al., 2022). Evidence of dehumanization can be seen in the over-disciplining and the policing of Black bodies in schools (Goff et al., 2014; Johnson et al., 2017). As part of the ubuntu principles, learning is enhanced and deepened via learners interacting with one another, allowing children to acquire skills, values, and attitudes in a classroom setting where they will share responsibility for their success (Maphalala, 2017). Accepting ubuntu requires rejecting Western Eurocentric worldviews as they demean African thought and uplift Whiteness (Maphalala, 2017).

In a community, it is essential to note that every member plays a vital role in its success. King & Swartz (2016) refers to the shared responsibility that is held as *communal responsibility.* Within communal responsibility, hierarchy of human worth is erased; therefore, everyone has a contribution to the community, and that contribution is equally valuable. This notion does not indicate that teachers relinquish their authority and responsibility as the adults in the classroom; rather, it honors the children's cultural knowledge, experiences, and input and is legitimate and valuable. Delpit (1988) explains that when teachers take on egalitarian or nonauthoritative roles, this does not remove authority but shifts the need to be in sole control. Rather than alienating children as the subordinate, creating a classroom community that is not authoritative in nature restores their humanity. As learners, children must take responsibility for ensuring that they are prepared and do their part in the learning process.

As communalism is built and maintained, communal responsibility brings forth the idea of reciprocity and is guided by the notion that the community is working toward a common goal while simultaneously ensuring the well-being of all on an individual and collective basis. Noting this, building community does not mean that there will be no misbehavior or other issues. Within a community, the responsibility is shared, and all must work to maintain and repair when necessary. As responsibility is shared, children will hold their peers accountable when appropriate and help guide them back to the community. Additionally, communal responsibility acknowledges that children, too, will be knowledge holders and sharers contributing to what King & Swartz (2016) identify as multiple ways of knowing.

Families are one example of communal living/existing. For some teachers, their classroom community becomes a family. This concept may not work for everyone, and it does not have to since communities comes in different variations based on their needs, personalities, and goals. When I was a teacher, there were some years when we were a family in that we operated in a community built and maintained on love, respect, and shared responsibility. Understanding families as a type of community helps deromanticize the idea of classrooms. I want to be abundantly clear that *creating a classroom community will not eliminate behavioral issues or create a utopia.* As in families, there will be times where there is agreement and times where there is tension in the group. The important part is grace, humanity, and forgiveness. Because the communities consist of humans, inevitably there will be times when all classroom values will not be upheld. In that case, there should be ways for individuals to make amends. I reflect on my time as a 4th-grade teacher in a classroom where we were a tight-knit family.

> Like any other family, we had our disagreements. What was essential was working through those disagreements and not allowing the

disagreements to destroy what was built. There were even moments I had to apologize. Exposing my humanity did not diminish my adulthood or pride; rather, it strengthened the trust within the community. Reassuring my efforts, one student shared, "you're the first teacher that just listened to me." (Jackson, 2023, p. 22)

BUILDING HEALTHY CLASSROOM COMMUNITIES

A healthy classroom community is not just a set of guidelines or values that say how members will behave; rather, it is comprised of three main components, (1) relationship, (2) environment, and (3) curricula. These three components account for a classroom community that is student centered, culture reflective, and has the goal of academic achievement and social and cultural competence.

Relationship

> "No significant learning can occur without a significant relationship."
> —Dr. James Comer

For Early Childhood practitioners, positive and healthy relationships with students are crucial as these relationships are critical to students' social development and will set the tone for school relationship (Lippard et al., 2018). Relationships are complex connections that are essential to a healthy teaching and learning space built on love. Not superficial love or generalized love; rather, "love connotes that all humans deserve the right to dignity, freedom, and equal opportunities" (Johnson et al., 2019, p. 48). Relationships are the foundation for both the student and the teacher.

Because of the complex nature of relationships, every student will not need the same things to be successful in a classroom. Some relationships will come naturally, while others will take some consistent work. Building relationships is about building respect, trust, and rapport (Hollie, 2017). What that will look like will differ depending on the individual. From a cultural understanding, there are some who approach respect in a hierarchal manner, meaning adults automatically get respect regardless of circumstances. In contrast, there are a number of people who adopt the idea of *mutual respect*, commonly stating "respect is earned, not given." If a teacher is accustomed to the hierarchal manner of respect, they may find difficulty in building positive relationships with students. Mutual respect honors the humanity in students without requiring the teachers (and other adults) to relinquish their authority. Building respect translates to trust and rapport. When a student has respect, trust, and rapport with a teacher, they are more receptive of their teaching and guidance. Rita Pierson (2013) puts it simply: "You know, kids don't learn from people they don't like."

Relationships with students are not the only relationships that are crucial. Familial relationships are just as important. Families, too, must trust that the teacher (and school) has their child's best interest at hand. Additionally, relationships are not one-sided; just as students and families will learn from the teacher, there are many things that teachers can learn from families. Families have rich knowledges that can support the teaching and learning happening in classrooms. Healthy relationships allow teachers to tap into that resource. In a complex world where we are teaching constrained relationships can be a source of hope for teachers, students, and families (Duncan-Andrade, 2007).

Environment

When relationships are strong, the environment reflects that. Students need an environment that they not only feel safe in, but that they are also affirmed in. The environment I am referring to allows students to be their authentic selves without anti-Black violence (Johnson et al., 2019). This includes but is not limited to being able to express themselves in words, fashion, and overall presentation, and being able to speak in home languages (such as African American Language) without being forced to always translate to Standardized English. I am referring to a place where what is on the walls is reflective of them. A place where they are required to be the best version of themselves with the supports they need to do so.

Curricula

Curricula/pedagogical violence is one of the five types of anti-Black violence Johnson et al. (2019) assert Black students experience in classrooms. Simply put, *what* teachers are teaching and *how* they are teaching it create barriers for students. Not only is it often not affirming, content and pedagogy practices uplift Whiteness and denote Blackness as an inferior way of being. Combating this violence, teachers can use strategies such as culturally relevant pedagogy (Ladson-Billings, 1995), culturally sustaining pedagogy (Paris, 2012), or African diaspora literacy (Boutte et al., 2017) to provide students with a learning experience that is relevant and affirming to them.

FROM RULES TO VALUES

As teachers think about their classroom communities, typically classrooms are guided by classroom rules. In this chapter, I guide readers from thinking about classroom *rules* to thinking about *value systems* that can be implemented. There is an adage I heard frequently growing up: Rules are meant to be broken. Hearing it, I chuckled because if often came from a person who was either being defiant or was planning to break a rule (or already had). This adage originally came from an American general, Douglas MacArthur. It has been shortened from his original statement, "Rules are mostly made to be broken and are too often for the lazy to hide behind."

Are rules really made to be broken, though? Why are rules even in place? Asking these questions doesn't imply that I think that people should have free rein to do whatever they would like. I do, in fact, think that there should be guidelines that we live by. In ancient Kemet (modern-day Egypt), Ma'at (discussed later in this chapter) was used a universal moral code that they believe brought order to human living (Karenga, 2003).

Rules are often in place under the notion of safety or to create some commonality or a standard. The issue arises in how rules in classrooms have mimicked laws and rules of stringent environments such as prisons. Typically prohibitive in nature, school rules often lead with "don't," and even when presented in a positive manner, they often limit students from doing basic things such as talking and interacting with peers. Many rules leave students to decide between following rules and satisfying the human need to commune with others. Hence, they are anti-communal in nature.

It is clear that rules are rooted in power. School rules that forbid impeding instructional time seek to control and manage children's behaviors. It seems to be beyond the realm of imagination that instruction should include open dialogue with and among children. Black children not only have to abide by the explicit rules that are put forth in classrooms, but they also must abide by the unwritten Eurocentric rules. Those unwritten rules create a different expectation for them and dictates how they speak, their tone, their body language, and how they can self-express, among other things. For example, African American Language (AAL) (discussed in Chapter 7) permits more than one person speaking at once (overlapping) or one person completing another person's sentence (conarration). Hence, Black children are likely to be reprimanded for a communication style that is permissible (and indeed expected) at home. This sort of unscaffolded responses to Black cultural ways of being deprives Black children of their youth and humanity. They are expected to navigate the world as an adult while only a child. Unwritten rules show up in teacher biases, assumptions, and increased expectations for Black children and are manifested through actions toward them.

The problem is that rules, explicit and implicit, often do not reflect the needs of children or help meet the goals of the classroom. Rather they are, whether by design or not, so prohibitive that they create a major hindrance to student success. Instead of rules, I encourage teachers to consider using value systems to guide the way classroom communities interact with each other. Value systems do not focus on what *not* to do; they provide a guide to show acceptable ways to interact. Further, values that are co-selected with children's input are more likely to result in a commitment and effort to meet the community's goals. It is essential that the values reflect the needs of the children in the classroom.

I share three African value systems that complement Pro-Black classrooms: (1) Adinkra symbols, (2) Ma'at, and (3) n'guzo saba. These value systems can be implemented in various ways to meet the requirements of schools and also the needs of particular classrooms. I provide a brief background overview of each of the value systems and suggested readings for further engagement. When engaging with Afrocentric practices, Akua (2020) suggests teachers immerse themselves in one practice and build a strong knowledge base rather than attempting to take small bites of many concepts.

Adinkra Symbols

As noted in Chapter 3, Adinkra symbols originate from the West African Akan people. These symbols were a part of a robust language and communication system that included verbal and nonverbal aspects. Originally used for royal families and funerals, these symbols have been used and are currently used in clothing, decorations, furniture, and other symbolisms. Adinkra symbols reflect "proverbs, historical events, plant life forms, and shapes of inanimate and man-made objects" (Kissi et al., 2019, p. 30). There are countless symbols, and their names and meanings may slightly differ depending on the source, but they are representative of the many ways to be and to believe in African culture. Values may also overlap, and the same value may be represented by different symbols (Jackson et al., 2021).

Adinkra symbols, while originating in modern-day Ghana and Côte D'Ivoire, have extended to countries where African diasporic people live. For example, in a recent Fulbright-Hays Group Abroad trip to Barbados, I noticed Adinkra symbols at the Rock Hall freedom village (Figure 9.2). The village, now a memorial park, was created

Figure 9.2. Bannisters at Rock Hall Freedom Village

Figure 9.3. Adinkra Symbol Sankofa Bird and Heart

by former slaves as the first freehold village in 1841. Today, the fence boldly features the symbols *nkonsonkonson* (unity), *boa me na me mmoa wo* (cooperation), *me ware wo* (commitment), and *owuo atwedee* (universality of death). We were not able to determine who included the symbols in the fence.

In the United States, the sankofa bird is a commonly known Adinkra symbol. The sankofa bird is a mythical creature that is forward facing, yet the head faces backwards with an egg in its mouth. This symbol represents learning from the past while moving forward. The egg represents protecting the children (see Figure 9.3).

An alternative design of sankofa that mimics a heart is commonly found in window gates and yard gates (see Figure 9.4).

Teachers have translated this value system in their classrooms in a variety of ways. For example, after introducing Adinkra symbols to students, I had each student pick a symbol to represent who they are and a value they would embody in our community. On a provided square, each student created what became a block on our classroom quilt. This activity was accompanied by the book *The Patchwork Quilt* (Flournoy, 1985), and I shared my experience with my grandmother making quilts. This "quilt" we created was a reminder of the values that we were committing to live by within our community. Adinkra symbols were not just our classroom community value system, they were also an analytical tool in which we evaluated behaviors and actions of those we learned about. For example, when introducing Black historical figures (individuals and groups of people), I shared symbols that represented values that

Figure 9.4. Window Gate on House in Barbados

I thought they embodied (see Figure 9.5). Students shared their thoughts on those symbols and added additional ones when fitting. This provided constant examples of how to personify Adinkra symbols in everyday life. It was also an opportunity to deepen our understanding of Black people and cultural themes on a common system of values.

When teachers find themselves in situations where rules or derivatives of them are provided by their schools or district, Adinkra symbols (or other value systems) can still be used. Ms. Janice R.

Figure 9.5. Slides Showing Black Historical Figures and Adinkra Symbols

Baines (featured in Chapter 6), in a 2nd-grade class, was a part of a school that used a program called *Leader in Me* (Covey, 2014). Part of the implementation of this schoolwide program was the adoption of *The Seven Habits of Happy Kids* (Covey, 2014). When introducing the habits, (Habit 1: *Be Proactive*; Habit 2: *Begin With the End in Mind*; Habit 3: *Put First Things First*; Habit 4: *Think Win-Win*; Habit 5: *Seek First to Understand, Then to Be Understood*; Habit 6: *Synergize*; and Habit 7: *Sharpen the Saw*), Ms. Baines facilitated a conversation with children about which Adinkra symbols represented the ideas of the principles. Based on their conversations, they matched each habit with an Adinkra symbol on a classroom poster (shown in Figure 9.6). Classroom posters were accompanied by individual posters, and children made pledges using "I" statements and making additional Adinkra symbols (Figure 9.6). Children's input increased their commitment to upholding the principles. Additionally, their interest was piqued as they gained cultural knowledge about Africa, not only in their classroom behavior but in academic lessons.

During Black History Month, Ms. Baines engaged children in an exploratory project called *Hidden Figures* where the students interviewed members of the school community including the principal, teachers, custodial staff, and support staff. This project was designed to honor and highlight "hidden" people in their school—people whose phenomenal work and impact are often overlooked. During interviews with teachers, children asked various curated questions and created artwork that included a picture that they created, an

Figure 9.6. Class Poster With Seven Habit and Adinkra Symbols

Figure 9.7. Class Bullentin Board With Student Projects

actual photo of the person, and a biography that contained various facts about their interviewee, including their favorite book and childhood game (shown in Figure 9.7). Students included an Adinkra symbol that they thought their interviewee portrayed. They were able to take all the information they learned during their interview to determine which Adinkra symbols their person embodies. In some cases, they were empowered through teaching their interviewee about Adinkra symbols.

I point this activity out to show the elasticity of implementing Adinkra symbols or other value systems. Activities may not always be elaborate, but including the value system among all aspects of the classroom community reinforces children's understanding and cultural competence. Moreover, I use this example to show the connection to state-mandated standards. For example, in this project Ms. Baines covered the following South Carolina standards:

> Standard 1: Meaning and Context (MC) Interact with others to explore ideas and concepts, communicate meaning, and develop logical interpretations through collaborative conversations; build upon the ideas of others to clearly express one's own views while respecting diverse perspectives.
> Standard 3: Communicate information through strategic use of multiple modalities and multimedia to enrich understanding when presenting ideas and information.

Many of the authors of this book use the Adinkra value system, and examples can be found embedded throughout this book. Additional examples can be found in "Back to Africa: Lessons from the Motherland" (Jackson et al., 2021).

Ma'at Principles

Ma'at of ancient Kemet (now Egypt) is the goddess of truth, justice, harmony, and balance dating back to 2375 BCE (Mark, 2016; Wynter-Hoyte & Smith, 2020). The values exhibited by this goddess translated into the concept of Ma'at. Ma'at was a response to chaos, providing a way by which the universe could be maintained in harmony and peace (Rosicrucian Egyptian Museum, n.d.). The virtues have been translated into 42 laws of Ma'at. These laws or principles are not directly recorded in historical documents but interpreted through anthropologists and historians who have studied ancient writings. The 42 laws of Ma'at have also been simplified to seven principles: truth, justice, balance, order, compassion, harmony, and reciprocity.

Similar to Adinkra symbols, Ma'at can easily align with schoolwide rules and expectations. In her African studies class Ms. Saudah N. Collins (Chapters 4 and 5) displays the seven principles and refers to them in conjunction with various topics throughout the year. Introducing the principles, Ms. Collins poses the question, "How do we create a space of peace and joy?" Children share their responses in drawings and with the class. She encourages them to think about the Ma'at principles not only in terms of their classroom community but also in their contributions to the world. Figure 9.8 shows a daily agenda for an introductory lesson on Ma'at.

Ms. Mukkaramah Smith and Dr. Kamania Wynter-Hoyte, a teacher and teacher educator pair, share examples in a 1st-grade class using Ma'at principles as a guide for classroom community and instruction (Wynter-Hoyte & Smith, 2020). Seeking a more substantial and culturally relevant rule system, Ms. Smith saw Ma'at as a moral code that the students could self-regulate (M. Smith, personal communication, August 8, 2023). Rather than traditional rules and behavior guidelines, Ms. Smith decided to introduce Ma'at principles using *Light as a Feather: The 42 Laws of Ma'at for Children* (Nebthet, 2015) as an anchor text. Other texts that supported

Figure 9.8. Photo of Ms. Collins Class Board With Agenda

teaching the principles included *Each Kindness* (Woodson, 2012) and *The Youngest Marcher* (Levinson, 2017). Figure 9.9 shows how a student responded to specific principles of Ma'at through the discussion. In it you will see the student made "I" statements showing their commitment to upholding the principles.

As a remedy to the displeasure with the school-provided behavior chart that kept track of negative behaviors, Ms. Smith decided to use Ma'at principles to transform the behavior chart to reflect positive behaviors. Understanding that adopting the Ma'at principles would not guarantee "perfect" behaviors, children also created consequences for when the principles were not followed. Interestingly, they chose not to be completely exclusionary. For example, instead of completely removing a child's chance to go to the treasure box if the principles were not followed, the child would be limited to a smaller prize rather than the cooler prizes (i.e., pencil, eraser, chip, or drink, instead of glow sticks, extra recess, or sitting with friends at lunch). Children are typically open to restorative disciplinary processes. They

Figure 9.9. Student Work of Maat Principles

implemented the need to apologize and share how the child who had done harm would change their behavior in order to rejoin the class (M. Smith, personal communication, August 8, 2023). Ultimately, children had a say in what the classroom community would look like and how it would look if wrong was done among the community, which gave them a sense of ownership. Wynter-Hoyte & Smith (2020) shared how they began to observe children exemplify the various principles, hold each other accountable, and explicitly make connections to their personal lives.

Nguzo Saba

Kwanzaa, an African American celebration observed December 26 to January 1 annually, was founded by Dr. Maulana Karenga. While frequently confused as an African holiday, Kwanzaa was a response to the experiences of Black people in the United States who suffered cultural trauma to provide a revival of histories and traditions (Karenga, 2006). Kwanzaa was a means to (re)member Black and African culture and identity amid social unrest in the United States (Hicks Tafari & Poole, 2016). Kwanzaa was and is a site of resistance—resistance to conformity to the dominant culture and identity. *Nguzo saba*, Swahili for the seven principles, guides the 7-day celebration. Karenga & Karenga (2007) describe nguzo saba as a "central value foundation and framework to undergird and inform our personal and collective practice as a people" (p. 21), stating they were "chosen with a critical appreciation for where we are now as a people and the particular challenges we face and must deal with successfully" (p. 22). Those principles, as presented by Karenga & Karenga (2007), are:

- *Umoja* (unity): "To strive for and maintain unity in the family, community, nation and race."
- *Kujichagulia* (self-determination): "To define ourselves, name ourselves, create for ourselves and speak for ourselves."
- *Ujima* (collective work and responsibility): "To build and maintain our community together and make our sister's and brother's problems our problems and to solve them together."
- *Ujamaa* (cooperative economics): "To build and maintain our own stores, shops and other businesses and to profit from them together."
- *Nia* (purpose): "To make our collective vocation the building and developing of our community in order to restore our people to their traditional greatness."
- *Kuumba* (creativity): "To do always as much as we can, in the way we can, in order to leave our community more beautiful and beneficial than we inherited it."
- *Imani* (faith): "To believe with all our heart in our people, our parents, our teachers, our leaders and the righteousness and victory of our struggle." (pp. 22–31)

While Kwanzaa is a once-a-year celebration, the values of nguzo saba can and should be upheld year-round. Each of the principles align to the idea of ensuring that the community and those in the community are at their peak wellness in body, mind, and spirit. Living in the values of nguzo saba is an example of living in ubuntu. In a classroom community, teachers can use nguzo saba as a value system that promotes personal and communal well-being socially, emotionally, and academically.

Table 9.1. Sample Texts That Describe Nguzo Saba

Principle(s)	Suggested Text
Kujichagulia (self-determination)	*Wilma Unlimited: How Wilma Rudolph Became the World's Fastest Woman* (Krull, 1996)
Umoja (unity)	*Sweet Clara and the Freedom Quilt* (Hopkinson, 1993)
Kujichagulia (self-determination)	
Ujima (collective work and responsibility)	
Kuumba (creativity)	
Nia (purpose)	*Amazing Grace* (Hoffman, 1991)
Ujamaa (cooperative economics)	*Uncle Jed's Barbershop* (Mitchell, 1998)

A common practice in classrooms is having a "morning meeting." When adopting nguzo saba in a classroom community, those meetings can be transformed to community meetings, family meetings, or even a umoja (unity) circle (Obijiofor, 2003). A multitude of things can occur during this time, including sharing Black and African cultural histories (Jackson, 2023), resolving conflict (Obijiofor, 2003), or simply setting the tone for the day.

Additionally, Obijiofor (2003) suggests texts that can be used with each of the seven principles (shown in Table 9.1). This list is not exhaustive but gives teachers a starting point.

Implementing any value system will require commitment from teachers. It requires becoming knowledgeable about the systems and thoughtful ways to meaningfully implement within occupied space. Teachers don't have to be experts, though, but should have a strong understanding and willingness to vulnerably assume the task of being a lifelong learner alongside children. Children will ask questions that will require research, which can be completed by the teacher or collectively in a learning journey.

OTHER CLASSROOM COMMUNITY STRATEGIES AND CONSIDERATIONS

Regardless of where a teacher is in their understanding, they must start somewhere. Teachers may pick up this text in the middle of the school year and be empowered to make a change without the ability to do a complete overhaul. Consider introducing any of the shared value systems (or others not mentioned) and find ways to make simple reminders throughout the day. For example, if nguzo saba is shared, make connections during conversations and lessons. Additionally, a few other communal-style strategies are shared that will help create and maintain classroom communities. These activities can be used in conjunction with value systems or alone.

Affirmations

Affirmations avow a sense of love, appreciation, and respect for a particular thing. They tap into the oral dimension of Black culture and the AAL communication call-and-response style. In this context, classroom affirmations can be individual or collective (or both). They are a reminder of who we are, our capabilities, and our commitment to a common purpose. Using affirmations is not new to education since teachers often use them to uplift and empower children. They are also used as a way for children to take pride in themselves and their abilities.

Inspired by a TED Talk with Rita Pierson, I incorporated a classroom affirmation with my students. After a few weeks of reciting it, the students no longer needed the poster (shown in Figure 9.10). "I am Somebody," it started, lived in and through the students in that classroom. I would occasionally hear students reciting it in the hallways, and it was posted as a reminder if ever faced with a challenging moment.

Call-and-Response

Call-and-response is a core tradition in Black culture. It is the act of a speaker making an assertion (call) and listeners responding (response). This can be in the form of agreement, an encouragement for the speaker to continue, or a completion of a sentence (Foster, 2002; Smitherman, 1977). Call-and-response can be seen in verbal interactions, music, and dance. It not only contributes to affirming classroom but supports students' academic success as reflected in higher reading scores on standardized tests (Foster, 2002). While teachers may use some form of call-and-response in most classrooms, I call attention to the use of affirming call-and-responses instead of generic

Figure 9.10. Classroom Affirmation Poster

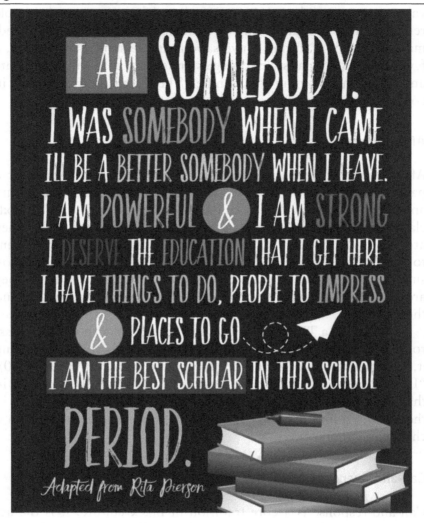

ones. For example, Saudah N. Collins (Chapter 5) says "class, class" and children respond "yes, yes."

Some teachers use "Agoo," garnering the response "Amee," a call-and-response in the Ghanian Twi language (Chapter 3). "Agoo" asks the audience for permission to speak, and "Amee" not only tells the speaker that they have the listener's attention but is reflected in the full attention of the responder (Boutte et al., 2017). Additional examples draw from current pop culture waves. For example, singer Beyoncé has created a challenge during her Renaissance World Tour. In her song ENERGY (Beyoncé, 2022), the lyrics "look around everyone on mute" (call) triggers a silence (response) until she continues singing. This could be used in classrooms and is likely to be appreciated by children who are Beyoncé fans. There are a myriad of examples from places of worship, social conversations, and other aspects of Black life that can be used to support a Pro-Black classroom community.

CONCLUSION

The very concept of management, as typically understood, can inadvertently strip away the humanity and agency of those involved. By framing classroom management in terms of control, we risk overshadowing the potential for children to actively contribute to their own growth and development. Creating and sustaining such classroom communities necessitates an ongoing commitment. Just as communities evolve over time, so do the individuals within them and their collective needs. This chapter's exploration of classroom communities, their purpose, and supporting literature pave the way for fostering environments that embrace the students we teach.

Several Pro-Black alternatives to typical "management" strategies were offered. Regardless of where a reader is in their understanding, in essence, this chapter serves as an impassioned call to action. It challenges educators to transform their spaces into affirming, inclusive, supportive, and empowering classroom communities. By embracing this holistic approach, we embark on a journey toward equity, respect, and Pro-Blackness.

Endnotes

Chapter 1: Pro-Blackness in Early Childhood Education

1. My grandchildren call me "Dear," which is short for "My dear."

Chapter 2: Amplifying Pro-Black Perspectives in Child Development

1. We are aware of separation of church and state and ask readers to understand that we are not suggesting indoctrination into any particular religion. We are recommending playing a *variety* of music, some of which may resonate with what children hear in their homes. This can be used a bridge for literacy and so much more.

2. A West African percussion instrument made of a dried gourd and a woven netting of beads.

3. Anthony Broughton is also a performer for children and has several children's books and videos. His pen/stage name is MISTER B. When he taught preschool, children also called him MISTER B. Additional information can be found at his website: Dr. Anthony Broughton. MISTER B (https://www.misterbinspires.com/).

Chapter 4: I'll Take You There

1. See Boutte (2022), Boutte et al. (2021b), Jackson et al., (2021) and Johnson et al. (2018a) for examples of a cadre of teachers engaged in African diaspora literacy instruction.

2. Word walls are used to build children's vocabulary throughout the year. Many times, the walls are started with just the letters of the alphabet. Ms. Collins used pages from the *Alphabet of Black Cultures* (Daniels, 2020) as the starting point for each letter.

3. Many people focus on animals when talking about Africa. This focus exoticizes Africa and dehumanizes the people who live there.

4. The *habitual be* in AAL references doing something in the past, present, and future—in perpetuity. Ms. Collins's message connotes that she has loved Black children in the past, she loves Black children presently, and she will love Black children in the future. This is everlasting love.

Chapter 6: Pro-Blackness as a Loving Antidote in Early Childhood Classrooms

1. I was part of a Fulbright-Hays Group Abroad project to Sierra Leone in 2011.

2. Kehinde Wiley is a contemporary artist who creates portraits using Black people. Smith, J. (2018). *A portrait of modern art: Exploring the works of Kehinde Wiley*. Art Publications.

3. This is the nickname for Dr. Boutte. "Dear" is short for "My Dear," which is what her biological and other "grandchildren" call her.

Chapter 8: What's Up, Fam (Family)?

1. South African concept called *ubuntu*.

2. The trips to Ghana and Cameroon were Fulbright-Hays Group Study Abroad experiences that require learning about the history, cultures, and practices of the countries.

References

Adamu, M., & Hogan, L. (2015). *Point of entry: The preschool-to-prison pipeline.* Center for American Progress.

Akbar, N. (2003). *Akbar papers in African psychology.* Mind Productions & Associates.

Akua, C. (2020). Standards of Afrocentric education for school leaders and teachers. *Journal of Black Studies, 51*(2), 107–127.

Alim, H. S., & Smitherman, G. (2012). *Articulate while black (Barack Obama, language, and race in the U.S.).* Oxford University Press.

Anderson, M. D. (2015). Why are so many preschoolers getting suspended? *The Atlantic.*

Baines, J., Tisdale, C., & Long, S. (2018). *We've been doing it your way long enough: Choosing the culturally relevant classroom.* Teachers College Press.

Baker-Bell, A. (2017). "I can switch my language, but I can't switch my skin": What teachers must understand about linguistic racism. In E. Moore, A. Michael, and M. W. Penick-Parks (Eds.), *The guide for White women who teach Black boys* (pp. 97–107). Corwin Press.

Battle-Lavert, G. (1994). *The barber's cutting edge.* Lee & Low Books.

Beyoncé. (2022). ENERGY [Song]. On *Renaissance.* Parkwood Entertainment and Columbia Records.

Bino and Fino. (2019, December 23). *Come on let's dance dance dance! Get the kids moving!* [Video]. YouTube. https://www.youtube.com/watch?v=EmAwTeFVlKA

Bishop, R. S. (1990). Mirrors, windows, and sliding glass doors. *Perspectives, 6*(3), ix–xi.

Blacktown Arts. (2020, May 11). *Drumming workshop for kids: Learn African dance steps to "A lion has a tail"* [Video]. YouTube. https://www.youtube.com/watch?v=U3A1s8S_fDY

Boutte, G. S. (2008). Beyond the illusion of diversity: How early childhood teachers can promote social justice. *Social Studies, 99*(4), 165–173.

Boutte, G. S. (2013). Teaching students who speak African American language: Expanding educators' and students' linguistic repertoires. In M. E. Brisk (Ed.), *Language, culture, and community in teacher education* (pp. 47–70). Routledge.

Boutte, G. S. (2015a). *Educating African American students: And how are the children?* Routledge.

Boutte, G. S. (2015b). Kindergarten through grade 3: Four things to remember about African American language: Examples from children's books. *YC Young Children, 70*(4), 38–45.

Boutte, G. S. (2016). *Educating African American students: And how are the children?* Routledge.

Boutte, G. S. (2017). Teaching about racial equity issues in teacher education programs. In S. M. Curenton, T. R. Durden, and I. U. Iruka (Eds.), *African American children in early childhood education* (pp. 247–266). Emerald Publishing Limited.

Boutte, G. S. (2022). *Educating African American students: And how are the children?* (2nd ed.). Routledge.

Boutte, G., & Baker-Bell, A. (2022). A conversation with Dr. Gloria Swindler Boutte and Dr. April Baker-Bell. *Talking Points, 33*(2), 2–10.

Boutte, G., & Bryan, N. (2019). When will Black children be well? Interrupting anti-Black violence in early childhood classrooms and schools. *Contemporary Issues in Early Childhood, 22*(3), 232–243.

Boutte, G. S., & Compton-Lilly, C. (2022). Prioritizing Pro-Blackness in literacy research, scholarship, and teaching. *Journal of Early Childhood Literacy, 22*(3), 323–334.

Boutte, G. S., Earick, M. E., & Jackson, T. O. (2021a). Linguistic policies for African American language speakers: Moving from anti-Blackness to pro-Blackness. *Theory Into Practice, 60*(3), 231–241.

Boutte, G. S., & Johnson Jr., G. L. (2013a). Do educators see and honor biliteracy and bidialectalism in African American language speakers? Apprehensions and reflections of two grandparents/professional educators. *Early Childhood Education Journal, 41*, 133–141.

Boutte, G. S., & Johnson Jr., G. L. (2013b). Funga Alafia: Toward welcoming, understanding, and respecting African American speakers' bilingualism and biliteracy. *Equity & Excellence in Education, 46*(3), 300–314.

Boutte, G. S., Johnson Jr., G. L., Wynter-Hoyt, K., & Uyoata, U. E. (2017). Using African diaspora literacy to heal and restore the souls of Black folks. *International Critical Childhood Policy Studies Journal, 6*(1), 66–79.

Boutte, G. S., King, J. E., Johnson Jr., G. L., & King, L. J. (Eds.). (2021). *We be lovin' Black children: Learning to be literate about the African diaspora.* Myers Education Press.

Boutte, G. S., & Strickland, J. (2008). Making African American culture and history central to teaching and learning of young children. *Journal of Negro Education, 77*(2), 131–142.

Boykin, A. W. (1978). Psychological/behavioral verve in academic/task performance: Pretheoretical considerations. *Journal of Negro Education, 47*, 343–354.

Boykin, A. W. (1983). The academic performance of Afro-American children. In J. Spence (Ed.), *Achievement and achievement motives* (pp. 324–337). Freeman.

Boykin, A. W. (1994). Afrocultural expression and its implications for schooling. In E. R. Hollins, J. E. King, & W. C. Hayman (Eds.), *Teaching diverse populations: Formulating a knowledge base* (pp. 243–273). State University of New York Press.

Boykin, A. W. (2001). Culture matters in psychosocial experience and schooling of African American students. Submitted for publication in the *Harvard Education Review.*

Boykin, A. W., & Cunningham, R. T. (2001). The effects of movement expressiveness in story content and learning context on the cognitive performance of African American children. *Journal of Negro Education, 32*, 256–263.

Boykin, A. W., Jagers, R. J., Ellison, C. M., & Albury, A. (1997). Communalism: Conceptualization and measurement of an Afrocultural social orientation. *Journal of Black Studies, 27*(3), 409–418.

Boykin, A. W., & Toms, F. D. (1985). Black child socialization: A cultural framework. In H. P. McAdoo & J. L. McAdoo (Eds.), *Black children: Social, educational, and parental environments* (pp. 33–51). Sage.

Brann, S. K., & Morales-James, C. (2023). *The ABCs of the Black Panther Party*. My Reflection Matters, LLC.

Bridges, R. (2009). *Ruby Bridges goes to school. My true story*. Scholastic.

Broughton, A. (2016). Where is my stuff? Conceptualizing hip hop as "play," *Early Child Development and Care, 187*(5–6), 869–877.

Broughton, A. (2019). *Evidence-based approaches to becoming a culturally responsive educator: Emerging research and opportunities*. IGI Global.

Broughton, A. (2022). Black skin, White theorists: Remembering hidden Black early childhood scholars. *Contemporary Issues in Early Childhood, 23*(1), 16–31. https://doi.org/10.1177/1463949120958101

Busia, A. (1989). What is your nation? Reconstructing Africa and her diaspora through Paule Marshall's Praisesong for the widow. In C. Wall (Ed.), *Changing our own words* (pp. 196–211). Rutgers University Press.

Chocolate, D. (1997). *Kente colors*. Walker Childrens.

Clark, K. B., & Clark M. P. (1947). Racial identification and preference in Negro children. In T. M. Newcomb and E. L. Hartley (Ed.), *Readings in social psychology*. Holt, Rinehart, and Winston.

Clark-Robinson, M. (2018). *Let the children march*. Clarion Books.

CNN Pilot Demonstration. (2010). http://i2.cdn.turner.com/cnn/2010/images/05/13/expanded_results_methods_cnn.pdf

Cline-Ransome, L. (2013). *Light in the darkness: A story about how slaves learned in secret*. Little, Brown Books.

Cline-Ransome, L. (2015). *Freedom's school*. Little, Brown Books for Young Readers.

Cole, J. B. (2021). *African proverbs for all ages*. Roaring Book Press.

Coleman, E. (1996). *White socks only*. Albert Whitman & Company.

Coles, R. (2010). *The story of Ruby Bridges*. Scholastic.

Constant, R. E., & Zeger, J. (2018). *Hey, Tuskegee!* Mascot Books.

Cook, M. (2012). *A celebration of Rosa, Barack, and pioneers of change*. Bloomsbury USA Childrens.

Cooke, T. (2008). *So much!* Candlewick.

Covey, S. R. (2014). *Leader in me*. Simon and Schuster.

Dance 'N' Culture. (2021a, February 19). *Dance for kids! | West African* [Video]. YouTube. https://www.youtube.com/watch?v=WWNWVDzLM9c

Dance 'N' Culture. (2021b, April 12). *Dance for kids! | Hip hop* [Video]. YouTube. https://www.youtube.com/watch?v=HhB15mbJ8ec

Daniels, J. (2020). *Alphabet of Black cultures*. Sleeping Elephant.

Deans, K. (2021). *Swing sisters: The story of the international sweethearts of rhythm*, Holiday House.

Delpit, L. D. (1988). The silenced dialogue: Power and pedagogy in educating other people's children. *Harvard Educational Review, 58*, 280–299.

Delpit, L. D., & White-Bradley, P. (2003). Educating or imprisoning the spirit: Lessons from ancient Egypt. *Theory Into Practice, 42*(4), 283–288.

Derman-Sparks, L., & Edwards, J. O. (2010). *Anti-bias education for young children and ourselves* (Vol. 254). National Association for the Education of Young Children.

Derman-Sparks, L., & Ramsey, P. G. (2006). *What if all the kids are White? Anti-bias multicultural education with young children and families.* Teachers College Press.

Dillard, C. B. (2012). *Learning to (re)member the things we've learned to forget: Endarkened feminisms, spirituality, & the sacred nature of research & teaching.* Peter Lang.

Dillard, J. L. (1972). *Black English.* Random House.

DjembeDirect. (2008, October 9). *Djembe—Making a djembe—Ghana, West Africa* [Video]. YouTube. https://www.youtube.com/watch?v=aLeede5z1vQ

Du Bois, W. E. B. (1903). *The souls of Black folk.* First Vintage Books, Library of America Edition.

Dumas, M., & Ross, K. (2016). "Be real Black for me": Imagining BlackCrit in education. *Urban Education, 5*(4), 415–442.

Duncan, A. F. (1995). *Willie Jerome.* Atheneum.

Duncan-Andrade, J. (2007). Gangstas, wankstas, and ridas: Defining, developing, and supporting effective teachers in urban schools. *International Journal of Qualitative Studies in Education, 20*(6), 617–638.

Earick, M. E. (2009). *Racially equitable teaching: Beyond the Whiteness of professional development for early childhood educators.* Peter Lang.

Educational Testing Services (ETS). (2019). *Praxis principles of learning and teaching: Grades K-6.* Educational Testing Service.

Eide, B., & Eide, F. (2006). *The mislabeled child.* Hyperion.

Emdin, C. (2016). *For White folks who teach in the hood . . . and the rest of y'all too: Reality pedagogy and urban education.* Beacon Press.

Fanon, F. (1952). The fact of blackness. *Postcolonial studies: An anthology, 15*(32), 2–40.

Fanon, F. (1963). *The wretched of the earth.* Grove.

Ferguson, P. V. (1896). Plessy v. Ferguson. *Retrieved from*: https://scholar.google.com/scholar?hl=en&as_sdt=0%2C34&q=plessy+v+ferguson+1896&btnG.

Flournoy, V. (1985). *The patchwork quilt.* Penguin.

Ford, D. Y., Grantham, T. C., & Whiting, G. W. (2008). Another look at the achievement gap: Learning from the experiences of gifted Black students. *Urban Education, 43*(2), 216–239.

Fordham, S. (1988). Racelessness as a factor in Black students' school success: Pragmatic strategy or Pyrrhic victory? *Harvard Educational Review, 58*(1), 54–85.

Foster, M. (2002). *Using call-and-response to facilitate language mastery and literacy acquisition among African American students.* ERIC Clearinghouse on Languages and Linguistics.

Fu-Kiau, K. K. B., & Lukondo-Wamba, A. M. (1988). *Kindezi: The Kongo art of babysitting.* Imprint Editions.

Gilliam, W. S. (2005). *Prekindergarteners left behind: Expulsion rates in state prekindergarten systems.* Foundation for Child Development.

Givens, J. (2019). "There would be no lynching if it did not start in the schoolroom"; Carter G. Woodson and the occasion of Negro History Week, 1926–1950. *American Educational Research Journal, 56*(4), 1457–1494.

GlobalWondersSeries. (2008, December 9). *Global wonders: Hello song with sing-a-long* [Video]. YouTube. https://www.youtube.com/watch?v=kjwkMmdqmH4

Goff, P. A., Jackson, M. C., Di Leone, B. A. L., Culotta, C. M., & DiTomasso, N. A. (2014). The essence of innocence: Consequences of dehumanizing Black children. *Journal of Personality and Social Psychology, 106*(4), 526–545. https://doi.org/10.1037/a0035663

Good Reads. (2023). Maya Angelou quotes. https://www.goodreads.com/quotes/7273813-do-the-best-you-can-until-you-know-better-then

Gregory, A., & Roberts, G. (2017). Teacher beliefs and the overrepresentation of Black students in classroom discipline. *Theory Into Practice, 56*(3), 187–194.

Hale, J. E. (2001). *Learning while Black: Creating educational excellence for African American children*. JHU Press.

Hale, J. E. (1982). *Black children: Their roots, culture, and learning styles*. Johns Hopkins University Press.

Hale-Benson, J. E. (1986). *Black children: Their roots, culture, and learning styles* (Rev. ed.). Johns Hopkins University Press.

Hannah-Jones, N. (2021). *The 1619 project: Born on the water*. Kokila.

Harris, J. C. (2008). *The classic tales of brer rabbit*. Running Press Kids.

Harris, V. J. (2007). In Praise of a scholarly force: Rudine Sims Bishop. *Language Arts, 85*(2), 153–159. https://experts.illinois.edu/en/publications/in-praise-of-a-scholarly-force-rudine-sims-bishop

Herring, M., Jankowski, T. B., & Brown, R. E. (1999). Pro-black doesn't mean anti-white: The structure of African-American group identity. *The Journal of Politics, 61*(2), 363–386.

Hicks Tafari, D., & Poole, T. (2016) The Kinara speaks: Kwanzaa as an expression of activism and resistance in the city of Greensboro. In R. Brock, D. Nix-Stevenson, & P. C. Miller (Eds.), *Critical Black studies reader*. Peter Lang.

Hilliard, A. G., III. (1991). Do we have the will to educate all children? *Educational Leadership, 49*(1), 31–36.

Hilliard, A. G., III. (1992). Behavioral style, culture, and teaching and learning. *The Journal of Negro Education, 61*(3), 370–377.

Hilliard, A. G., III. (1995). *The maroon within us: Selected essays on African American community socialization*. Black Classic Press.

Hilliard, A. G., III. (2002). *African power: Affirming African indigenous socialization in the face of the culture wars*. Makare Publishing.

Hines, E. M., Ford, D. Y., Fletcher Jr., E. C., & Moore III, J. L. (2022). All eyez on me: Disproportionality, disciplined, and disregarded while Black. *Theory Into Practice, 61*(3), 288–299.

Hoffman, M. (1991). *Amazing grace*. Scholastic.

Hollie, S. (2017). *Culturally and linguistically responsive teaching and learning: Classroom practices for student success*. Shell Educational Publishing.

Hopkinson, D. (1993). *Sweet Clara and the freedom quilt*. Knopf.

Howard, T. C. (2010/2019). *Why race and culture matter in schools: Closing the achievement gap in America's classrooms*. Teachers College Press.

Igus, T. (1998). *I see the rhythm*. Children's Book Press.

Jackson, J. J. (2023). Starting with the man in the mirror: A Black male teacher's use of African diaspora literacy to reckon with Black consciousness. *Social Studies and the Young Learner, 35*(3), 20–25.

Jackson, J. J., Collins, S. N., Baines, J. R., Boutte, G. S., Johnson Jr., G. L., & Folsom-Wright, N. (2021). Back to Africa: Lessons from the motherland. *Social Studies, 112*(3), 120–135.

Johnson, A. (2007). *A sweet smell of roses*. Simon & Schuster Books for Young Readers.

Johnson, D. (1998). *All around town: The photographs of Richard Samuel Roberts*. Henry Holt and Co.

Johnson, L. L., Boutte, G. S., Greene, G. R., & Smith, D. (2018a). *African diaspora literacy: The heart of transformation in K-12 schools and teacher education*. Lexington Books.

Johnson, L. L., Bryan, N., & Boutte, G. (2019). Show us the love: Revolutionary teaching in (un)critical times. *Urban Review, 51*(1), 46–64.

Johnson, L. L., Jackson, J., Stovall, D. O., & Baszile, D. T. (2017). "Loving Blackness to death": (Re)imagining ELA classrooms in a time of racial chaos. *English Journal*, 60–66.

Jools TV. (2022, May 25). *Affirmations | JOOLS TV Trapery Rhymes* [Video]. YouTube. https://www.youtube.com/watch?v=Qe_5XP5wslo

Jordan, J. (1970). Afterword. In J. Jordan & T. Bush (Eds.), *The voice of the children* (pp. 92–98). Holt, Rinehart, & Winston.

Jordan, J. (1988). Nobody mean more to me than you and the future life of Willie Jordan. *Harvard Educational Review, 58*(3), 363–375.

Karenga, M. (2003). *Maat: The moral ideal in ancient Egypt: A study in classical African ethics*. Routledge.

Karenga, M. (2006). *The message and meaning of Kwanzaa: Bringing good into the world*. University of Sankore Press.

Karenga, M., & Karenga, T. (2007). The nguzo saba and the Black family: Principles and practices of well-being and flourishing. In H. P. McAdoo (Ed.), *Black families* (pp. 19–33). Sage Publications.

Kennedy Center Education Digital Learning. (2012a, June 4). *Five(ish) minute dance lesson—African dance: Lesson 3: Dancing on the clock* [Video]. YouTube. https://www.youtube.com/watch?v=Ewqq-3xJFdI

Kennedy Center Education Digital Learning. (2012b, June 4). *Five(ish) minute drum lesson—African drumming: Lesson 1: The djembe* [Video]. YouTube. https://www.youtube.com/watch?v=q5U8md4rZS8

King, J. E. (1992). Diaspora literacy and consciousness in the struggle against miseducation in the Black community. *Journal of Negro Education, 61*(3), 317–340.

King, J. E. (2005). *Black education: A transformative research and action agenda for the new century*. Routledge.

King, J. E., & Maïga, H. O. (2018). Teaching African language for historical consciousness: Recovering group memory and identity. In J. E. King & E. E. Swartz (Eds.), *Heritage knowledge in the curriculum* (pp. 56–78). Routledge.

King, J. E., & Swartz, E. E. (2014). *"Re-membering" history in student and teacher learning. An Afrocentric culturally informed praxis*. Routledge.

King, J. E., & Swartz, E. E. (2016). *The Afrocentric praxis of teaching for freedom: Connecting culture to learning*. Routledge.

King, J. E., & Swartz, E. (2018). *Heritage knowledge in the curriculum: Retrieving an African episteme*. Routledge.

King, L. J. (2020). Black history is not American history: Toward a framework of Black historical consciousness. *Social Education, 84*(6), 335–341.

Kissi, S. B., Fening, P. A., & Asante, E. A. (2019). The philosophy of Adinkra symbols in Asante textiles, jewelry, and other art forms. *Journal of Asian Scientific Research, 9*(4), 29.

Kohlberg, L., & Turiel, E. (1971). Moral development and moral education. In G. S. Lesser (Ed.), *Psychology and educational practice* (pp. 410–465). Scott, Foresman & Company.

Krull, K. (1996). *Wilma unlimited: How Wilma Rudolph became the world's fastest woman*. Harcourt Brace.

Ladson-Billings, G. (1995). Toward a theory of culturally relevant pedagogy. *American Educational Research Journal, 32*, 465–491.

Ladson-Billings, G. (2006). From the achievement gap to the education debt: Understanding achievement in U.S. schools. *Educational Researcher, 35*(7), 3–12.

Ladson-Billings, G. (2017). The (r)evolution will not be standardized: Teacher education, hip hop pedagogy, and culturally relevant pedagogy 2.0. In D. Paris & S. Alim (Eds.), *Culturally sustaining pedagogies: Teaching and learning for justice in a changing world* (pp. 141–156). Teachers College Press.

Ladson-Billings, G. (2018). Foreword. In J. E. King & E. E. Swartz (Eds.), *Heritage knowledge in the curriculum: Retrieving an African episteme* (pp. x–xii). Routledge.

Ladson-Billings, G. (2022). *The dreamkeepers: Successful teachers of African American children* (2nd ed.). Jossey-Bass.

Lawrence, J. (1995). *The great migration: An American story*. HarperCollins.

Legette, K. B., Rogers, L. O., & Warren, C. A. (2022). Humanizing student–teacher relationships for Black children: Implications for teachers' social–emotional training. *Urban Education, 57*(2), 278–288.

Levinson, C. (2017). *The youngest marcher: The story of Audrey Faye Hendricks, a young civil rights activist*. Simon and Schuster.

Levy, Y. (2018). "Developmental delay" reconsidered: The critical role of age-dependent, co-variant development. *Frontiers in Psychology, 9*, 503.

Lewis, A. D., & Taylor, N. A. (2019). *Unsung legacies of educators and events in African American education*. Palgrave Macmillan.

Lippard, C. N., La Paro, K. M., Rouse, H. L., & Crosby, D. A. (2018, February). A closer look at teacher–child relationships and classroom emotional context in preschool. *Child & Youth Care Forum, 47*, 1–21.

Long, S., Baines, J., & Tisdale, C. (2018). *"We've been doing it your way long enough": Choosing the culturally relevant classroom*. Teachers College Press.

Love, B. L. (2016). Anti-Black state violence, classroom edition: The spirit murdering of Black children. *Journal of Curriculum and Pedagogy, 13*(1), 22–25.

Love, B. L. (2019). *We want to do more than survive: Abolitionist teaching and the pursuit of educational freedom*. Beacon Press.

Lyons, K. S. (2012). *Ellen's broom*. G. P. Putnam's Sons Books for Young Readers.

Maphalala, M. C. (2017). Embracing ubuntu in managing effective classrooms. *Gender and Behaviour, 15*(4), 10237–10249.
Mark, J. J. (2016, September 15). Ma'at. *World History Encyclopedia.* https://www.worldhistory.org/Ma'at/
Mase. (2004). Welcome back [Song]. On *Welcome cack.* Bad Boy.
McDermott, G. (1987). *Anansi the spider: A tale from the Ashanti.* Henry Holt and Company.
McKissack, P. (1986). *Flossie and the fox.* Dial Books.
Medearis, A. S. (1994). *Our people.* Atheneum.
Miller, Jr. E. A. (2008). *Gullah statesman. Robert Smalls from slavery to Congress, 1839–1915.* University of South Carolina Press.
Milner IV, H. R. (2012). Beyond a test score: Explaining opportunity gaps in educational practice. *Journal of Black Studies, 43*(6), 693–718.
Milner IV, H. R., Cunningham, H. B., Delale-O'Connor, L., & Kestenberg, E. G. (2018). *"These kids are out of control": Why we must reimagine classroom management for equity.* Corwin Press.
Mirror of Race. (2023). *True pictures.* http://mirrorofrace.org/true-pictures/
Mitchell, M. K. (1998). *Uncle Jed's barbershop.* Aladdin.
Mitchell, R. (1997). *The talking cloth.* Scholastic.
Monroe, C. R. (2005). Understanding the discipline gap through a cultural lens: Implications for the education of African American students. *Intercultural Education, 16*(4), 317–330.
Muller, M., Braden, E. G., Long, S., Boutte, G. S., & Wynter-Hoyte, K. (2022). Toward pro-Black early childhood teacher education. *Young Children, 77*(1), 44–51.
Musgrove, M. (1992). *Ashanti to Zulu: African Traditions.* Puffin Books.
Musgrove, M. (2015). *The spider weaver: A legend of kente cloth.* Apprentice House.
Myer, S. L. (2016). *New shoes.* Holiday House.
Myers, W. (1997). *Harlem. A poem by Walter Dean Myers.* Scholastic.
Ndlovu Youth Choir. (2020, September 21). *Ndlovu Youth Choir—Jerusalema Dance Challenge* [Video]. YouTube. https://www.youtube.com/watch?v=IlGlmAGskGc
Nebthet, K. (2015). *Light as a feather: 42 laws of Ma'at for children.* Ra Sekhi Arts Temple.
Nobles, W. W. (1976). Extended self: Rethinking the so-called Negro self-concept. *Journal of Black Psychology, 2*(2), 15–24.
Noguera, P. (2008). *The trouble with Black boys: Reflections on race, equity and the future of public education.* Wiley and Sons.
Nuurali, S. (2022). *The tortoise and the hare: A West African graphic folktale.* Picture Window Books.
Obama, B. H. (2013, December 10) *Remarks by President Obama at memorial service for former South African president Nelson Mandela* [Speech]. Obama White House Archives. https://obamawhitehouse.archives.gov/the-press-office/2013/12/10/remarks-president-obama-memorial-service-former-south-african-president-
Obijiofor, C. L. (2003). Connecting Kwanzaa and literature to build a classroom community. *Reading Teacher, 57*(3), 287–290.

Ofori, I. E. (2020). *Princess Akoto: The story of the golden stool and the Ashanti kingdom*. Tellwell Talent.
Owusu, P. (2019). Adinkra symbols as "multivocal" pedagogical/socialization tool. *Contemporary Journal of African Studies*, 6(1), 46–58.
Paris, D. (2012). Culturally sustaining pedagogy: A needed change in stance, terminology, and practice. *Educational Researcher*, 41(3), 93–97.
Philadelphiatribune. (2019, December 1). *Black fathers build bonds through ballet dancing* [Video]. YouTube. https://www.youtube.com/watch?v=p6lZl7Xc_KM
Pickney, B. (1997). *Max found two sticks*. Aladdin Books.
Pierson, R. (2013). Every kid needs a champion. *TED Talks Education*.
PINK THUMB Pre-K & Kindergarten Learning Channel. (2021, February 21). *Who am I? A positive affirmation poem in honor of Black History Month and everyday* [Video]. YouTube. https://www.youtube.com/watch?v=DPaK6BI0obI
Robinson, A. (2020). *The modern day Black alphabet*. Lyn-111.
Rosales, M. B. (1996). *'Twas the night before Christmas: An African-American version*. Cartwheel Books.
Rosicrucian Egyptian Museum. (n.d.). *Ma'at*. Deities in ancient Egypt—Ma'at. https://egyptianmuseum.org/deities-Maat
Segura-Mora, A. (2008). What color is beautiful? In A. Pelo (Ed.), *Rethinking early childhood education* (pp. 3–6). Rethinking Schools.
Serramo, A., & Toepke, A. (Co-Directors). 1998. *The language you cry in* [Film]. Elphinstone Institute. https://www.imdb.com/title/tt0157919/
Shade, B. J. (1997). *Culture, style, and the educative process: Making schools work for racially diverse students* (2nd ed.). Charles T. Thomas.
Sharma, S. (2019). Decolonizing the mind: The politics of language, culture and identity. *International Journal of Research and Analytical Reviews*, 6(2), 225–227.
Singham, M. (2003). The achievement gap: Myths and reality. *Phi Delta Kappan*, 84(8), 586–591.
Smalls, I. (2004). *Don't say ain't*. Charlesbridge.
Smith, J. (2018). *A portrait of modern art: Exploring the works of Kehinde Wiley*. Art Publications.
Smitherman, G. (1977). *Talkin and testifyin: The language of Black America*. Wayne State University Press.
Smoke, D. (2020). Black habits I. [Song]. On *Black habits*. WoodWorks Records.
Staple Singers. (1972). I'll take you there [Song]. On *Be altitude: Respect yourself*. Stax Records.
Tatum, B. D. (2007). *Can we talk about race? And other conversations in an era of school resegregation*. Beacon Press.
Tchana, K. (2002). *Sense Pass King: A Story from Cameroon*. Holiday House.
Turner, A. (2015). *My name is truth: The life of Sojourner Truth*. Harper Collins.
Vasquez, M. J. (2007). Cultural difference and the therapeutic alliance: An evidence-based analysis. *American Psychologist*, 62(8), 878.
Venter, E. (2004). The notion of ubuntu and communalism in African educational discourse. *Studies in Philosophy & Education*, 23(2/3), 149–160. https://doi.org/10.1023/B:SPED.0000024428.29295.03
Vernon-Jackson, H. (2012). *West African folk tales*. Courier Corporation. Little, Brown Books.

Wa Thiong'o, N. (1981). *Decolonizing the mind.* James Currey.
Weatherford, C. B. (2007). *Freedom on the menu. The Greensboro sit-ins.* Puffin Books.
Webber, T. L. (1978). *Deep like the rivers: Education in the slave quarter community, 1831–1865.* Norton.
Weatherford, C. B. (2006). *Moses: When Harriet Tubman led her people to freedom.* Little Brown Books for Young Readers.
Weatherford, C. B. (2021). *Unspeakable: The Tulsa race massacre.* Carolrhoda Books.
Weiss, G. D., & Thiele, B. (1995). *What a wonderful world.* Atheneum Books.
Winter, J. (1992). *Follow the drinking gourd.* Dragonfly.
Wilson, A. N. (1992). *Awakening the natural genius of Black children.* Afrikan World InfoSystems.
Wilson, A. N. (1978). *The developmental psychology of the Black child.* African Research Publications.
Wilson, S. M., & Peterson, P. L. (2006). *Theories of learning and teaching: What do they mean for educators?* National Education Association.
Winter, J. (2008). *Wangari's trees of peace: A true story from Africa.* Harcourt Children's Books.
Wonder, S. (1991, May 28). These three words [Song]. On *Jungle Fever.* American R&B.
Woodson, C. G. (1933/1990). *The mis-education of the Negro.* Africa World Press.
Woodson, J. (2012). *Each kindness.* Penguin Young Readers Group.
Wright, B. L., & Counsell, S. L. (2018). *The brilliance of Black boys: Cultivating school success in the early grades.* Teachers College Press.
Wright, B. L., Cross, B., Ford, D., & Tyson, C. (2022). When I think of home: Black families supporting their children during the COVID-19 pandemic. *Education and Urban Society, 55*(5), 515–532. https://doi.org/10.1177/00131245211065415
Wynter-Hoyte, K., & Smith, M. (2020). "Hey, Black child. Do you know who you are?" Using African diaspora literacy to humanize blackness in early childhood education. *Journal of Literacy Research, 52*(4), 406–431.
Zumba. (2022, May 13). *Zumba® Latin Easy-to-Follow Basic Steps Tutorial for Beginners* [Video]. YouTube. https://www.youtube.com/watch?v=e5rW7qjd3BY

Index

The ABCs of the Black Panther Party (Brann), 68
Academic literature, 149–150
Adamu, M., 41
Adinkra symbols, 55, 61, 69, 78, 83–85, 94, 159–164
  akoma, 117–119
  Black historical figures and, 161
  for interconnectedness, 98, 102
  at Rock Hall Freedom Village, 159–160
  sankofa, 57, 119–122, 160
Advancement Via Individual Determination (AVID) program, 80–81
Affect, 44–47, 59
Affirmations, 96–108, 169, 170
Affirmations: JOOLS TV Trapery Rhymes (song), 97
African American cultural dimensions, 28–34, 58–60, 152
  affect, 44–47
  communalism, 38–39
  harmony, 42–44
  integration of, 79–80
  spirituality, 34–38
  verve, 40–42
African American imagery, 115–117
African American Language (AAL), 6–7, 13, 79, 125–147
  as co-parallel language, 128–129
  policies and assessments, 129
  speakers, 128–129, 130–131
African diaspora literacy (ADL), 14–16, 73–74, 111, 112
  exploring Pro-Blackness through, 89–108

  extrapolating, 23
  interlocking components of, 16
  pedagogies and methodologies, 16–23
  shaping classroom with, 113–114
African diasporic decor, 115–117
African natural resources slide, 64
African Proverbs for All Ages (Cole), 36
African values and principles, 22
Agoo (Akan term), 55
Akbar, N., 27, 43, 45
Akoma, 117–119, 160
Akua, C., 159
Akwaaba, 76, 95–96, 111, 143–144
Albury, A., 152
Alim, H. S., 125
All Around the Town. The Photographs of Richard Samuel Roberts (Johnson), 67
Amee (Akan term), 55
Anansi the Spider: A Tale From the ASHANTI (McDermott), 63
Ancient Africa and the African continent, 57, 62–63
Anderson, M. D., 150
Anti-Blackness, 8–9
  defined, 9–10
  impact on young children, 11–14
  violence, 12–14
Anti-slavery campaign, 65
Asante, E. A., 159
The Atlantic (Anderson), 150

Baines, J. R., 16, 46, 48, 55, 72, 73, 79, 83, 114, 143, 159, 164
Baker-Bell, A., 126, 128, 129

The Barber's Cutting Edge (Battle-Lavert), 130
Baszile, D. T., 12, 153
Battle-Lavert, G., 130
Beyoncé, 171
Bishop, R. S., 76, 90, 110
Black-affirming spaces, 74
Black agency, 18–19
Black cultural dimensions, 22
Black families, 133–147
  dynamic/diverse, 136–137
  honoring and understanding, 137–143
  voices, hearing and honoring, 144
Black Greek Letter Organizations (BGLO), 77
Black historical consciousness themes, 17–22
Black historical contention, 21–22
Black identities, 20–21
Black joy, 20
#BlackLivesMatter movement, 9, 10
Black nationalist, 67–68
Black Nationalist movement, 5
Blackness, 7, 8
  power of, 92–96
Black Pages (publication), 136–137
Black theories, 47–48
Boutte, G. S., 7, 10, 11, 12, 15, 16, 17, 19, 21, 22, 23, 25, 26, 28, 41, 45, 47, 48, 55, 57, 61, 72, 73, 74, 77, 79, 80, 83, 86, 90, 91, 92, 109, 110, 111, 113, 115, 123, 128, 129, 143, 151, 155, 156, 157, 159, 164, 170
Boykin, A. W., 8, 16, 22, 27, 28, 29, 34, 37, 39, 40, 41, 44, 45, 47, 48, 80, 152
Boyles, W., 51
Braden, E. G., 45
Brann, S. K., 68
Bridges, R., 68
Broughton, A., 27, 45, 46, 47, 48, 52, 123
Brown, R. E., 7
Bruner, J., 39
Bryan, N., 12, 26, 91, 123, 128, 151, 155, 156, 157
Busia, A., 15

Call-and-response, 169–171
Center for the Education and Equity of African American Students (CEEAAS), 74, 75, 110
Charles, R., 5
Chocolate, D., 19, 63
Civil Rights era, 57, 67–68
Clark, K. B., 46
Clark, M. P., 46
Classroom management
  defined, 150–151
Cline-Ransome, L., 18, 60, 65, 66
Coles, R., 18, 68
Collins, S. N., 16, 55, 72, 73, 83, 143, 159, 164
Communalism, 38–39, 59, 152–155
Communal responsibility, 153
Compton-Lilly, C., 7, 10, 109
Constant, R. E., 77
Contemporary life in African diaspora, 57, 68–69
Cook, M., 20
Cooke, T., 130
Counsell, S. L., 40, 41
Covey, S. R., 162
Crosby, D. A., 155
Cross, B., 45
Culotta, C. M., 153
Cultural continuity, focusing on, 54–55
Cultural dimensions, African American. *See* African American cultural dimensions
Cultural values, 8
Cunningham, H. B., 149
Cunningham, R. T., 41
Curricular violence, 13, 157

Dance, 80, 99–100
Daniels, J., 173
Deans, K., 67
Dehumanization, 153
Delale-O'Connor, L., 150
Delpit, L. D., 35, 154
Derman-Sparks, L., 17, 46
Dewey, J., 39
Diaspora literacy
  African. *See* African diaspora literacy (ADL)
  defined, 15

Di Leone, B. A. L., 153
Dillard, C. B., 79, 80
Dillard, J. L., 125–126
DiTomasso, N. A., 153
Don't Say Ain't (Smalls), 131
Double Conscious play, 46
Drs. Diaspora curriculum, 51–52
  background, 56–57
  components of, 54–56
  description of, 57–62
  overview of, 52–54
Drs. Diaspora Kente Mystery Bag, 63
Duality of socialization, 46
DuBard, Keda, 146–147
Du Bois, W. E. B., 26, 45
Dumas, M., 9, 45
Duncan, A. F., 130
Duncan-Andrade, J., 156

Each Kindness (Woodson), 165
Earick, M. E., 9, 110, 115, 128
Early Childhood (EC) teachers, 25–26, 47
  role of, 1
Edwards, J. O., 17, 46
Eide, B., 40
Eide, F., 40
Ellen's Broom (Lyons), 66
Ellison, C. M., 152
Emdin, C., 47
Enslavement, 64–65
Environment, for healthy classroom community, 156
Expressive individualism, 59

Families
  Black. *See* Black families
  and learning spaces, 92–93
Fanon, F., 45
Fening, P. A., 159
Ferguson, P. V., 46
Fletcher, E. C., Jr., 150
Flocabulary, 66
Flossie and the Fox (McKissack), 131
Flournoy, V., 160
Floyd, George, 10

Folsom-Wright, N., 16, 55, 72, 73, 83, 143, 159, 164
Ford, D. Y., 45, 72, 150
Fordham, S., 127
Foster, M., 169
Freedom's School (Cline-Ransome), 66
Fu-Kiau, K. K. B., 42

Gilliam, W. S., 10, 41
Givens, J., 12
Goff, P. A., 153
Grantham, T. C., 72
The Great Migration: An American Story (Lawrence), 67
Greene, G. R., 28
Gregory, A., 150
Grief, sharing, 36
Gullah Statesman: Robert Smalls From Slavery to Congress (Miller), 67
Gye w'ani (Adinkra symbols), 83

Hale, J. E., 26
Hale-Benson, J. E., 22, 28, 29, 30, 31, 33, 36, 37, 39, 40, 41, 43, 44, 45, 46
Hannah-Jones, N., 19, 65
Hari bibi (Black water), 8
Harlem. A Poem by Walter D. Myers (Myers), 67
Harlem Shake, 100
Harmonious classrooms, 43–44
Harmony, 42–44, 58
Harris, J. C., 59
Harris, V. J., 90
Healing, through learning, 110–113
Healthy classroom community
  environment, 156
  relationship, 155–156
Herring, M., 7
Hey Tuskegee (Constant & Zeger), 77
Hicks Tafari, D., 166
Hilliard, A. G., III, 8, 22, 28, 29, 30, 31, 33, 34, 35, 37, 39, 40, 43, 45, 48
Hines, E. M., 150
Historical and contemporary perspectives, 23

Historically Black Colleges and Universities (HBCUs), 77
Historical periods, in United States, 57
   Ancient Africa and the African continent, 57, 62–63
   Civil Rights era, 57, 67–68
   contemporary life in African diaspora, 57, 68–69
   enslavement, 57, 64–65
   Jim Crow era, 57, 67
   reconstruction, 57, 65–67
Hoffman, M., 168
Hogan, L., 41
Hollie, S., 155
Hopkinson, D., 168
Howard, T. C., 72

Igus, T., 60
"I'll Take You There" (Singers), 71
Imani (faith), 167
Improvisation, 60
Individualism, expressive, 59
In My Africa (YouTube video), 62
Interconnectedness, Adinkra symbols for, 98, 102
Interdependence/oneness, 43
International Decade for People of African Descent (2015–2024), 10

Jackson, J. J., 12, 16, 54, 55, 72, 73, 83, 143, 153, 155, 159, 164, 168
Jackson, M. C., 153
Jackson, T. O., 110, 115, 128
Jagers, R. J., 152
Jankowski, T. B., 7
Jim Crow era, 57, 67
Johnson, A., 18, 68
Johnson, D., 67
Johnson, G. L., Jr., 16, 55, 72, 73, 83, 128, 143, 159, 164
Johnson, L. L., 12, 28, 91, 151, 153, 155, 156, 157
Jordan, J., 14, 79

Karenga, M., 157, 167
Karenga, T., 167

Kente Colors (Chocolate), 63
Kestenberg, E. G., 149
King, J. E., 8, 15, 16, 22, 55, 72, 73, 80, 111, 153, 154
King, L. J., 16, 17, 19, 20, 21
Kissi, S. B., 159
Kohlberg's theory of moral development, 35
Krull, K., 168
Kujichagulia (self-determination), 167
Kuumba (creativity), 167
Kwanzaa, 166–167

Labu bibi (Black earth), 8
Ladson-Billings, G., 16, 26, 41, 48, 72, 90, 157
Lady Justice, 35
La Paro, K. M., 155
Lawrence, J., 67
Leader in Me (Covey), 162
Legette, K. B., 153
Let the Children March (Clark-Robinson), 68
Levinson, C., 165
Levy, Y., 40
Lewis, A. D., 26, 48
Light as a Feather: The 42 Laws of Ma'at for Children (Nebthet), 164
Light in the Darkness. A Story About How Slaves Learned in Secret (Cline-Ransome), 65
Linguistic violence, 13
Lippard, C. N., 155
Long, S., 45, 46, 48, 72, 73, 79, 114
Love, B. L., 12, 26, 45
Lukondo-Wamba, A. M., 42
Lyons, K. S., 66

Ma'at principles, 164–166
Maïga, H. O., 8
Mandela, N., 101, 153
Maphalala, M. C., 152, 153
Mark, J. J., 164
McDermott, G., 19, 63
McKissack, P., 131
Medearis, A. S., 19, 62
Miller, E. A., Jr., 67
Milner, H. R., IV, 72, 149

Mirror of Race (website), 65
The Miseducation of the Negro (Woodson), 86
MISTER B's class, 42–43
Mitchell, M. K., 168
Mitchell, R., 62
Monroe, C. R., 150
Moore, J. L., III, 150
Moral development, 35
More knowledgeable other (MKO), 37
Movement, African American cultural dimensions, 57
Muller, M., 45
Musgrove, M., 19, 63
Music, 80, 99–100
Myers, W. D., 19, 67
My Family, My Culture, 137
My name is truth: The life of Sojourner Truth (Turner), 67

Name placards, 61–62
Natural resources slide, 64
Nea onnim no sua a, ohu (Adinkra symbols), 83
Nebthet, K. N., 19, 38
New Shoes (Myers), 67
Nguzo saba, 166–167
Nia (purpose), 167
Nobles, W. W., 43
Noguera, P., 40, 41
Nuurali, S., 36

Obama, B. H., 153
Obijiofor, C. L., 168
Ofori, I. E., 19
Oppression, 46
  power and, 17–18
Oral tradition, 59
Our People (Medearis), 62
Owusu, P., 83

Paris, D., 41, 157
The Patchwork Quilt (Flournoy), 160
Pedagogical violence, 13–14, 157
Perseverance, 18–19, 60
Peterson, P. L., 26

Physical violence, 12–13
Pierson, R., 156
Places, with African-descendant people, 52–53
Poole, T., 166
Power, and oppression, 17–18
PRAXIS test, 26
Pro-Black decor in classroom, 76–78
Pro-Black methodologies, 9
Pro-Blackness
  in early childhood education, 5–23, 74–85
  exploring through African diaspora literacy, 89–108
  power of, 110–113
Pro-Blackness, in early childhood classrooms, 109–122
  healing through learning, 110–113
  meaning of, 109–110
Pro-Black pedagogies, 1, 9, 10, 27, 73
  and content, 80–85
Pro-Black perspectives in child development, 27–47
  affect, 44–47
  communalism, 38–39
  harmony, 42–44
  spirituality, 34–38
  verve, 40–42
Pro-Black spaces
  African diaspora literacy and, 73–74
  creation of, 85–87
  Pro-Blackness in ECE settings, 74–85
  researcher positionality, 72–73
Proverbs, 36–37, 159

Ramsey, P. G., 46
Reconstruction, 65–67
Relationships, 155–156
Re-membering, 79, 111
Researcher positionality, 72–73
Resistance, 18–19
Roberts, G., 150
Robinson, A., 69
Rogers, L. O., 153
Rosales, M. B., 131
Ross, K., 9, 45
Rouse, H. L., 155

*Ruby Bridges Goes to School:
My True Story* (Bridges), 68
Rules, school, 157–159

Sankofa, 57, 119–122, 160
Schizoid play, 46
School rules, 157–159
Segura-Mora, A., 12
Self-concept development, 46
The Seven Habits of Happy Kids
(Covey), 162
Shade, B. J., 28
Sharma, S., 127
Singham, M., 72
The 1619 Project: Born on the Water
(Hannah-Jones and), 63
Smalls, I., 131
Smith, D., 28
Smith, J., 173
Smith, M., 114, 123, 164, 166
Smitherman, G., 125, 169
Smoke, D., 113
Social and emotional learning (SEL),
44–45
Social identity development, 46
Socialization, duality of, 46
Social time perspective, 60
So Much (Cooke), 130
The Souls of Black Folk (Du Bois),
26–27
South Carolina, 101
standards, 163–164
*The Spider Weaver: A Legend of Kente
Cloth* (Musgrove), 63
Spirituality, 34–38, 58
Standardized English (SE), 126
The Story of Ruby Bridges (Coles), 68
Stovall, D. O., 12, 153
Swartz, E. E., 8, 15, 16, 22, 80, 111,
153, 154
A Sweet Smell of Roses (Johnson), 68
Swing Sisters (Deans), 67
Symbolic violence, 13
Systemic school violence, 14

Talking Cloth (Medearis), 62–63
Tatum, B. D., 45
Taylor, N. A., 26, 48

Tchana, K., 58
Theory Into Practice (Gregory &
Roberts), 150
"These Three Words" (song), 117–118
Thiele, B., 58
Timelines
Tisdale, C., 46, 48, 72, 73, 79, 114
Toms, F. D., 45
"The Tortoise and the Hare" (Nuurali),
36
Turner, A., 67
'Twas the Night Before Christmas
(Rosales), 131
Tyson, C., 45

Ubuntu (South African philosophy), 27,
92, 94–95, 134–136, 153
Ujamaa (cooperative economics), 167
Ujima (collective work and
responsibility), 167
Umoja (unity), 167
University of South Carolina
(USC), 66
*Unspeakable: The Tulsa Race
Massacre* (Weatherford), 67

Value systems, 157
Vasquez, M. J., 40
Venter, E., 152, 153
Vernon-Jackson, H., 58
Verve, 40–42, 59
Violence, anti-Black, 151
curricular, 13, 157
linguistic, 13
pedagogical, 13–14, 157
physical, 12–13
symbolic, 13
systemic school, 14
Vygotsky, L., 37, 39

Wangari's Trees of Peace, 106–108
Warren, C. A., 153
Wa Thiong'o, N., 127
Watson, R., 19, 65
Wayne bibi (Black sun), 8
Weatherford, C. B., 67
W. E. B. Du Bois Center in Accra,
Ghana, 111, 112

We Be Lovin' Black Children: Learning to Be Literate About the African Diaspora (Boutte et al.), 6–7
Weiss, G. D., 58
"We Shall Overcome" (songs), 67–68
White-Bradley, P., 35
White privilege, 48
White Socks Only (Coleman), 68
Whiting, G. W., 72
Why Race and Culture Matter in Schools (Howard), 150
Willie Jerome (Duncan), 130–131

Wilson, A. N., 7, 8, 29, 30, 31, 33, 35, 41, 45, 46, 48
Wilson, S. M., 26
Wonder, S., 117, 118
Woodson, C. G., 19, 23
Woodson, J., 165
Wright, B. L., 40, 41, 45
Wynter-Hoyte, K., 45, 114, 123, 164, 166

The Youngest Marcher (Levinson), 165

Zeger, J., 77